Corporate Acquisitions and Mergers in Argentina

Corporate Acquisitions and Mergers in Argentina

Second Edition

Pablo Artagaveytia
Gabriel Gotlib

Marval, O'Farrell & Mairal

This book was originally published as a chapter in Corporate Acquisitions and Mergers.

General Editor: Peter Begg

Wolters Kluwer

Published by:
Kluwer Law International B.V.
PO Box 316
2400 AH Alphen aan den Rijn
The Netherlands
E-mail: international-sales@wolterskluwer.com
Website: lrus.wolterskluwer.com

Sold and distributed in North, Central and South America by:
Wolters Kluwer Legal & Regulatory U.S.
7201 McKinney Circle
Frederick, MD 21704
United States of America
Email: customer.service@wolterskluwer.com

Sold and distributed in all other countries by:
Air Business Subscriptions
Rockwood House
Haywards Heath
West Sussex
RH16 3DH
United Kingdom
Email: international-customerservice@wolterskluwer.com

Printed on acid-free paper

ISBN 978-94-035-0973-0

e-Book: ISBN 978-94-035-1012-5
web-PDF: ISBN 978-94-035-1060-6

This title is available on www.kluwerlawonline.com

Printed in the United Kingdom.

MARVAL, O'FARRELL & MAIRAL

Marval, O'Farrell & Mairal is the largest law firm in Argentina and a market leader at both local and Latin American levels. With over 300 lawyers, the firm has been providing sophisticated, high-quality advice to international and local clients for over ninety-five years on international business issues and the complexities of cross-border transactions. Marval is in the general practice of law including: banking and finance; capital markets; project finance; commercial and competition law; corporate law; foreign investments; mergers and acquisitions; real estate and construction law; administrative law; entertainment and media; environmental law; insurance law; intellectual property; internet and information technology; natural resources; utilities and energy law; tax and customs law; and telecommunications and broadcasting. The firm ranks at the top of major legal publications and has been awarded many international awards. *Chambers & Partners* recently recognized Marval as 'Argentina Law Firm of the Year 2018'.

Authors

Pablo A. Artagaveytia joined Marval, O'Farrell & Mairal in 1995 and became a partner of the firm in 2000. His area of specialization is centred on commercial and corporate law.

His professional work includes all areas of commercial law, advising on stock purchase agreements, distribution agreements, legal auditing, structuring of local companies, foreign business operations and general legal assistance, particularly focusing on the Mercosur region. In 1998 and 1999 he seconded Marval in the Brazilian firm Demarest & Almeida.

Before joining the firm he was a member Estudio de los Dres. O'Farrell between 1990 and 1994 and a court clerk in the National Civil and Commercial Courts from 1986 until 1990.

In 1990 he was an assistant professor of Commercial Law at the Schools of Law and Economics of the Universidad de Buenos Aires.

He graduated as a lawyer from the Universidad de Buenos Aires in 1990, and in 1995 he obtained a Master in International Law from the Southern Methodist University (Dallas, Texas, USA).

Gabriel Gotlib has been a member at Marval, O'Farrell & Mairal since 1997 and a partner since 2000. He specializes in tax, corporate and financial law.

He has broad experience in tax counselling, advising banks and local and foreign companies of different areas of practice such as real estate, retail and software. He also has experience advising on financing and international transactions and M&A.

Before joining the firm he worked for Ernst & Young LLP New York as an Argentine representative at the international tax planning headquarters from 1994 until 1995, at Ernst & Young's offices in Buenos Aires from 1995 until 1997, and at Carregal & Funes de Rioja in 1997. He has been an external advisor of the

Federal Government in reforms related to taxation of financial activities and international transactions.

He was a professor of Taxation of Financial Instruments at the Universidad de Buenos Aires School of Economics' Postgraduate Course on Taxation, and he is a professor of Tax Planning at the Austral University School of Law's Postgraduate Course on Taxation. He is the author of the books *Tax Litigation*, *New financial instruments*, *International Aspects of Argentine Tax System*, and *Myth of Tax Interpretation*.

Both a lawyer and certified public accountant from the University of Buenos Aires in the years 1990 and 1991, respectively, he also graduated from the International Tax Program (ITP) at the Harvard University School of Law in 1994.

He is a member of the International Fiscal Association and was the Argentine Reporter for the International Fiscal Association Congress held in Munich in 2000 on the topic of the taxation of hybrid instruments.

He is a member of the Academic Committee for the Master in Tax Law programme at Universidad Torcuato Di Tella (UTDT).

Contents

LOCAL ECONOMIC, POLITICAL AND CULTURAL ASPECTS

General Comments on the Country Profile

[01] The Republic of Argentina is comprised of twenty-three provinces and the Federal Capital: the Autonomous City of Buenos Aires. Located at the extreme south-east of the South American continent, Argentina is the eighth largest country in the world and the second largest in Latin America, covering some 3.8 m square kilometres (1.5 m square miles).

[02] Argentina has an estimated population of approximately 44.8 m people, of which 14.9 m live in the City of Buenos Aires and the greater Buenos Aires area. The overall population density is about sixteen persons per square kilometre. The population growth was of 126% from 1950 to date. Pursuant to the last census carried out in 2010, the illiteracy rate has been decreasing considerably in the past years and is currently at 1.9%.

[03] The official language is Spanish and the official currency is the Argentine Peso.

Legal System

[04] Argentina is organized as a federal republic with a democratic political system. The Argentine Constitution, adopted in 1853, provides in its present form for a tripartite system of government consisting of an executive branch headed by the president, a legislative branch and a judiciary.

[05] The executive branch has been the dominant branch at the federal level. The president is elected by direct vote and may serve a maximum of two consecutive, four-year terms.

[06] The Argentine Congress comprises two houses: the Senate and the House of Representatives, which constitute the legislative branch. Congress has exclusive power to enact laws concerning federal legislation, including international and inter-provincial trade, immigration and citizenship, patents and trademarks. The Argentine Constitution entitles Congress to enact the codes concerning civil, commercial, criminal, mining, labour and social security matters, which are applicable throughout the country.

[07] The judicial system is divided into federal and provincial courts, and each system has lower courts, Courts of Appeals and Supreme Courts. The supreme judicial power of Argentina is vested in the Argentine Supreme Court of Justice.

[08] Finally, each province enacts its own Constitution, elects its own governor and legislators, and appoints its own judges to the provincial courts.

Economic Aspects

[09] Argentina has a market-oriented economy with abundant natural resources, a well-educated population, an export-oriented agricultural sector and a relatively diversified industrial base.

[10] The *services* sector is the largest contributor to the total gross domestic product (GDP), accounting for over 60% of the economy and 72% of employment. Manufacturing represents 21% of GDP and 13% of employment, and agriculture represents 9% of GDP, generating 7% of employment. Construction, mining, public utilities and the service industry divide the rest.

[11] Regarding foreign trade, Argentine exports are fairly well diversified. However, although agricultural raw materials are over 20% of the total exports, agricultural goods still account for over 50% of exports when processed foods are included. Soy products alone (soybeans, vegetable oil) account for almost one-fourth of the total. Industrial goods today account for over a third of Argentine exports. Motor vehicles and auto parts are the leading industrial export and account for over 12% of the total merchandise exports.

[12] Finally, Argentina has the second-highest Human Development Index and GDP per capita in purchasing power terms in Latin America. Argentina is one of the G20 major economies, with the world's twenty-fourth largest nominal GDP, and is the twenty-third largest by purchasing power. The country is classified as upper-middle income or a secondary emerging market by the World Bank.

Cultural Aspects

[13] Argentine culture has been significantly influenced by Europe. In accordance with this, Buenos Aires, its cultural capital, is largely characterized by both the prevalence of people of European descent (mainly Italian and Spanish) and of a conscious imitation of European styles in architecture. The other big influence is their traditional country lifestyle of self-reliance, mainly represented in the archetypal figure of the 'gaucho'. Finally, indigenous American traditions (like yerba mate infusions) have been absorbed into the general cultural milieu.

[14] As regards popular culture, football stands out as the most popular sport. Furthermore, visual arts and literature also enjoy remarkable transcendence. These two fields of art have gained not only local but also international recognition along the years, with the most faithful representatives being Antonio Berni and Jorge Luis Borges, respectively. Lastly, local music is also highly acclaimed, with tango, *milonga* and *folclore* (folk music) as the main banners.

Background on Foreign Investment and M&A Activity in Argentina

[15] During the 1990s Argentina received a considerable flow of investment as a result of a process of liberalization and stabilization in the country's economy.

[16] Incoming venture capital was mainly placed in equity investments in large and medium-sized local corporations. Most of the transactions in those years consisted of private purchases of the controlling stock of companies, that is, without a public offer of acquisition through the capital market. This was due to the nature of most Argentine companies, which were typically family-owned.

[17] This tendency coincided with the privatization of state-owned utilities, which in turn boosted the M&A market throughout the country. Later, multinational companies bought up national private companies on a large scale. In general they were seeking the fastest way of expanding their businesses; instead of setting up a new company, they valued the advantages of companies that had already been built up. These included technical and market know-how, patents, permits and licenses and a complete storage and distribution network.

[18] During 2001 and 2002, Argentina went through one of the worst economic, political and social crises of its history. As a result of the crisis, the legal scenario of the prior decade was abruptly modified: freezing of bank deposits, devaluation, change of monetary system, reinstatement of exchange controls, and so on.

[19] One of the most important changes is the passing of the Law No. 25,561 of Public Emergency and Reform of the Exchange System (the Emergency Law) whereby the convertibility principle, based on the pegging of the peso to the dollar at a rate of ARS1 = USD1, which had been in place for almost eleven years, was abandoned.

[20] The Emergency Law abrogated the 'convertibility' of the peso into dollars and introduced the 'pesification' (*pesificación*) of certain US dollar or foreign currency denominated obligations.

[21] Argentina has an open attitude toward foreign investment, with few restrictions on foreign ownership. However, foreign exchange regulations apply which in some cases, do apply certain restrictions to acquisitions of companies or businesses that are engaged in particular areas of activity or in defence or national security concerns.

[22] Except for those special restrictions detailed hereunder, there are no general restrictions on foreign acquisition of Argentine enterprises. However, the Antitrust Law requires that notice of certain transactions such as mergers, transfers of businesses, acquisitions of shares or any other rights that confer control to the acquirer on the acquisition of assets of a company that are transferred to a person or economic group must be submitted to the pertinent governmental authority for clearance. The regulations apply to both foreign and domestic investors.

[23] Mergers and acquisitions are generally made on an agreed basis in Argentina. Agreed acquisitions by foreign investors have been common in the last decade while hostile bids have been rare. During the last two decades, there has been substantial growth in the number of overseas enterprises investing in Argentina. The main areas where foreign investment has been targeted are energy, international financial services (banks), telecommunications, pharmaceuticals, healthcare, supermarkets and consumer products.

Foreign Investment Legal Framework

[24] Foreign investments in Argentina are regulated by a framework of international treaties and Argentine laws that establish the norms for choice of law and jurisdiction, legal treatment of foreign investors, monetary policy and foreign exchange.

[25] In general, foreign investors wishing to invest in Argentina, either by starting up new businesses or by acquiring existing businesses or companies, do not require prior government approval except for regulated areas or for generally applicable regimes such as antitrust regulations. However, if a foreign company's investment consists of holding equity of an Argentine company, the foreign company must register with the Public Registry of Commerce (PRC) of the jurisdiction where the Argentine company is incorporated and comply with certain periodic reporting requirements.

[26] Foreign investments are governed by the Argentine Foreign Investments Law No. 21,382 enacted in 1976, which has subsequently been the subject of considerable amendment, with a view to liberalizing the regime applicable to them.

[27] The law states, as a general principle, that foreigners investing in economic activities in Argentina enjoy the same status and have the same rights that the Argentine Constitution affords local investors. Both are entitled to select any legal organization permitted by law and to have free access to domestic and international financing.

[28] A foreign investment sector that is still restricted to foreign investment is 'broadcasting'. However, there are certain Investment Protection Treaties executed between Argentina and third countries that may be construed to supersede such restriction (e.g., Investment Protection Treaty executed between Argentina and the United States of America). Also, Law No. 25,750, published in the Official Gazette on 7 July 2003 establishes that foreign ownership of media companies, directly or indirectly, is restricted to up to 30% of its shareholding or voting rights. Said percentage of foreign participation may be increased in case of reciprocity in the percentage permitted by the foreign country for the foreign investment in its media companies according to its legal framework. Further, Law No. 25,750 establishes that the following shall be considered media companies: (i) Newspapers, magazines and editorials companies. (ii) Broadcasting companies (television, radio, complementary broadcasting services providers, etc.). (iii) Producers of audiovisual and digital contents. (iv) Internet services providers. (v) Public booth advertisement companies.

[29] In addition Law No. 26,737 enacted in December 2011 imposes limits on the ownership or possession of rural land by foreign individuals or legal entities. For example, no more than 15% of the total amount of 'rural lands' in Argentine territory may be owned or possessed by foreign individuals or legal entities. This percentage is also applicable to the territory of the province or municipality where the relevant lands are located. Under no circumstance may foreign individuals or legal entities of the same nationality hold or possess more than 30% of the above-stated 15%. Also, ownership by the same foreign owner may not exceed one thousand hectares (1 000 ha) of the 'core area' or the 'equivalent surface' to be determined by the enforcement agency according to the location of the land.

[30] Lastly, foreigners who wish to purchase land located in frontier and other security areas, or who have a controlling participation in a company owning such land, must obtain prior government approval, which is usually obtained.

THE REGULATORY FRAMEWORK

Business Vehicles

[31] The most important forms of business vehicles in Argentina are the *Sociedad Anónima* (Argentine corporation with limited liability, hereinafter *SA*) and the *Sociedad de Responsabilidad Limitada* (Argentine limited liability company, hereinafter *SRL*). A recent reform that entered into force on 1 August 2015 introduced a new form of business organization: *Sociedad Anónima Unipersonal* (Argentine single shareholder corporation with limited liability, hereinafter *SAU*). The Argentine Companies Law No. 19,550, as amended (*CL*) provides the legal framework applicable to SAs, SRLs and SAUs.

[32] While the SA is the investment vehicle normally utilized by larger business enterprises, the SRL is now being employed more frequently by large undertakings. Considering its strict and costly requirements it seems that SAUs will be adopted by multinational enterprises for their wholly-owned subsidiaries. SRLs have traditionally been regarded as a vehicle suitable for small size businesses. However, there is at present an increasing interest in utilizing SRLs for larger enterprises, mainly because SRLs are required to comply with a smaller number of corporate formalities and are, in general, easier to administer than SAs. In addition, though SAs, SAUs and SRLs are subject to a substantially similar tax treatment, some foreign companies may find investment in SRLs advantageous due to 'pass through' tax benefits.

Sociedad Anónima

Shareholders: Capital

[33] Under Argentine law, an SA must be formed with a minimum of two shareholders that can be either legal entities or individuals. Since there are no nationality or residence requirements, foreign individuals (whether resident in Argentina or not) or non-Argentine companies may hold up to 100% of the share capital.

[34] Where the shareholders of the SA are Argentine companies, the CL sets forth an ownership limit by which domestic companies may not hold a participation in other companies greater than 100% of their voluntary reserves and 50% of their capital and legal reserves, if their corporate purpose is not exclusively that of a holding company or financial entity.

[35] The minimum capital required is ARS100 000. While the share capital of SAs must be fully subscribed upon incorporation, only 25% needs to be paid in at the time of subscription of the shares, and the balance within the following two years. Capital contributions of real estate, equipment or other non-monetary assets must be made in full upon subscription. Services do not qualify as capital contributions in the case of SAs. Non-monetary assets must be clearly identified and be of a type that can be subject to a judicial lien. The law provides rules with respect to asset valuation.

[36] Capital contributions other than in cash frequently face problems with respect to asset valuation. Such circumstances complicate and delay the incorporation process of a company. For this reason, companies are sometimes incorporated with a low capital paid in cash which is increased after the company has completed the incorporation process, through the contribution of the non-monetary assets, thereby avoiding delays in incorporation which may complicate the start-up of the project.

Shares: Transferability – Rights

[37] The capital of the SA is divided into shares, which are always of equal face value and expressed in Argentine currency. Argentine law does not permit companies to issue bearer shares. Shares may be either registered non-endorsable shares or book-entry shares. Share certificates may represent one or more shares.

[38] An SA may have different classes of shares with different rights attached to each class which in turn may be common (*acciones ordinarias*) or preferred (*acciones preferidas*). Common shares may give the holder the right to cast from one to five votes, as provided for in the by-laws. However, the issue of common shares granting the right to cast multiple votes (up to five) may grant economic preferences. Listed companies cannot issue shares with rights to cast multiple votes. Preferred shares may be non-voting except with respect to decisions on certain important matters such as the extension of the corporation's term, conversion into another type of entity except in the case of listed companies, fundamental change of the corporate purpose and transfer of the domicile of the corporation to another country. Non-voting shares gain the right to vote during the time in which the corporation is in default as regards the benefits attaching to their preference, or if the company is listed, for the period during which listing is suspended or withdrawn.

[39] Transfers of shares are generally unrestricted, but restrictions may be included in the by-laws provided that they do not effectively prevent the transfer of shares. Notice of transfers of shares must be provided to the board of directors. Such transfers, as of the time they are recorded in the share registry book, are effective vis-à-vis the company and third parties.

[40] The transferability of shares in an SA is governed by the company's by-laws. Provisions are often included giving existing shareholders a right of first refusal to purchase shares offered for transfer. Such provisions do not apply to transfer of shares in listed companies. Furthermore, even where no restrictions on transferability are set out in the by-laws of a company, shareholders' agreements frequently exist, under which parties to the agreement regulate the manner in which their voting rights may be exercised and grant pre-emptive rights to the other parties to the agreement in the event of a proposed transfer of shares of the company. While such agreements may be an obstacle in a take-over, they are not enforceable against third parties. Shareholders' agreements relating to unlisted companies need not be disclosed and are not public documents.

[41] SAs that publicly offer securities are subject to the rules of the National Securities Commission (*Comisión Nacional de Valores* or 'CNV' after its acronym in Spanish). The CNV requires the filing of copies of shareholders' agreements and notice must be given to the relevant stock exchange where such companies' securities are listed.

[42] In the event of a capital increase, a holder of existing shares of a given class (or of common shares in the event the capital is not divided into classes of shares) has a pre-emptive right (except in listed companies) to subscribe for a number of shares of the same class sufficient to maintain the holder's existing proportionate holdings of shares of that class. Pre-emptive rights (*derecho de preferencia*) also apply to the issue of convertible securities. Shareholders who have exercised their pre-emptive rights are entitled to accretion rights (*derecho de acrecer*) in proportion to their respective holdings with respect to non-pre-empted shares.

[43] Pre-emptive rights can be restricted in limited cases as provided by law. An extraordinary shareholders' meeting, with special majority requirements provided in the law, may decide on the restriction or suspension of pre-emptive rights in the subscription of new shares, if necessary for the company's interest, and subject to the following conditions: (i) that the need for such decisions be included on the agenda of the shareholders' meeting; (ii) that the shares to be issued be paid in kind or be given in payment of pre-existing obligations. Likewise, the Corporate Bonds Law No. 23,576 provides for additional cases where pre-emptive rights may be restricted or suppressed.

Registration, Annual Fees and Corporate Books

[44] An SA must be registered with the *PRC* of the jurisdiction of its legal domicile of incorporation (i.e., the City of Buenos Aires or any of the provinces). An SA registered with the PRC of the City of Buenos Aires must pay an annual fee, the amount of which shall vary according to the corporate capital of the SA as detailed in the last balance sheet filed with the PRC of the City of Buenos Aires.

[45] The following resolutions must be registered with the PRC: (i) the appointment, removal or resignation of members of the board of directors; (ii) the change of the legal domicile (registered office); (iii) any amendment to the by-laws; (iv) any increase in the corporate capital; and (v) any corporate reorganization.

[46] The SAs must file its annual financial statements with the PRC together with the 'annual reports' prepared by the board of directors, and if applicable, by the statutory supervisor.

[47] An SA with corporate capital exceeding the sum of ARS10 m must notify the PRC of its annual ordinary shareholders' meeting prior to holding any such meeting.

[48] Foreign entities that are shareholders of a local company must register their by-laws, any amendments thereof and other incorporation documents with the PRC.

[49] SAs must keep the following corporate books: 'share registry book'; 'attendance record book of shareholders' meetings'; 'minute book of the board of directors and of shareholders'; and, if applicable, 'minute book of the supervisory committee'. In addition, accounting books must be kept.

Management: Board of Directors

[50] The SA is managed by a single director or by a board of directors, as set forth in the by-laws. A minimum of three directors is required if the company's capital exceeds the sum of ARS10 m. Employees have no right to representation on the boards of Argentine companies.

[51] If the capital of the corporation is divided into different classes of shares, the by-laws may provide that each class elect one or more directors and establish the rules for such election.

[52] Directors, who need not be shareholders, are elected by the ordinary shareholders' meeting, to hold office for a period not exceeding three fiscal years, and may be re-elected.

[53] The majority of directors must reside in Argentina, regardless of their nationality. Therefore, all directors (and even the president) may be foreigners or nationals, provided that there is a majority of directors who are Argentine residents. All directors must have a special domicile in Argentina where notices must be given and process served in all matters relating to the SA.

[54] The board must meet at least once every three months and its quorum is the absolute majority of the directors. Unless a higher majority is provided for in the by-laws, decisions are taken by the majority of directors present at any meeting. In principle, the law requires that actual physical meetings be held, as opposed to telephone conferences, for which purpose at least members of the board constituting the quorum must be present. However, in recent years, the PRC has allowed meetings to be held through videoconferences if such alternative is provided for in the by-laws.

[55] The president, elected from among the members of the board, has full powers of representation. The president's powers in relation to third parties cannot effectively be limited by the by-laws. Restrictions on the president's powers cannot be invoked vis-à-vis third parties.

[56] The position of director of a company is exercised personally and cannot be delegated. However, a member of the board can give a proxy to another member of the board to vote on his or her behalf, provided that there is a quorum. At the same time, the board, as a body, may grant specific or broad powers of attorney to members of the board, officers or third parties. The board may also delegate certain administrative functions by appointing managers, who need not be directors. Within the board, committees may be created to deal with specific issues such as technical matters, financial matters, etc.

[57] Directors' remuneration may not exceed 25% of profits if dividends are paid or 5% of profits if no dividends are paid. Under special circumstances the ordinary shareholders' meeting may authorize a higher remuneration.

Directors' Liability

[58] Directors of SAs are subject to a standard of loyalty and diligence; non-compliance with this standard results in unlimited, joint and several liability for damages arising therefrom. Directors have the duty (a) to reveal any conflict of interest to the board of directors and the statutory supervisors; (b) to abstain from any deliberation related thereto; and (c) to refrain from competing with the company.

[59] Directors are unlimitedly, jointly and severally liable to the corporation, the shareholders and third parties for the negligent performance of their offices, for violations of the law or of the by-laws of the company and for any other damages caused by the director's fraud, gross negligence or abuse of authority.

[60] Directors, who file in a timely manner written objections to the corporate resolution that caused the damages and promptly give notice to the statutory supervisors before the proceedings are initiated against decisions of the board of directors, are exempt from any consequences arising from the resolution. Directors may be released from liability for certain decisions by a subsequent approval of the shareholders' meeting, provided that such decisions do not violate the law or the by-laws, and that shareholders representing 5% or more of the company's capital do not object.

Shareholders' Meetings

[61] Shareholders' meetings must take place at the company's registered office or within the jurisdiction of its legal domicile, and are either ordinary (*Asamblea Ordinaria*) or extraordinary (*Asamblea Extraordinaria*).

[62] Ordinary meetings must be called at least once a year, within four months from the end of the fiscal year, to consider the following matters: (i) financial statements, annual reports and distribution of profits; and (ii) appointment and removal of directors and statutory supervisors and their performance and fees.

[63] Extraordinary meetings are required to consider the amendment of by-laws and any other matters that are not among those items to be considered by law by ordinary meetings. In particular, extraordinary meetings are empowered to consider: (i) capital increases; (ii) capital reduction and capital refund; (iii) redemptions of shares; (iv) mergers, dissolutions, liquidations and spin-offs; (v) limitation or suspension of pre-emptive rights in subscription for new share issues; (vi) the issuance of debentures and their conversions into shares; and (vii) the issuance of bonds.

[64] Ordinary and extraordinary meetings must be held when called by the directors or statutory supervisors or by shareholders representing 5% of authorized capital unless the by-laws permit a smaller number.

[65] Notices of meetings are given by means of announcements published for five days in the Official Gazette, at least ten days in advance of the date specified for the holding of the meeting. However, no publications are necessary when all shareholders are present and decisions are taken unanimously.

[66] Shareholders may be represented by proxy at any meeting. Nevertheless, directors, managers, statutory supervisors and employees of the company may not represent shareholders.

[67] Quorum for ordinary meetings on first call requires the presence of a majority of shares with a right to vote. Ordinary meetings shall be deemed to be constituted on second call regardless of the number of shares present. Extraordinary meetings require, on first call, a quorum of 60% of shares with a right to vote unless the by-laws require a higher percentage and, on a second call, a quorum of 30% of voting shares unless the by-laws require a lower or a higher percentage. A majority of votes present at ordinary or extraordinary meetings is sufficient to carry a resolution unless the by-laws require a higher number.

[68] If a quorum is not present at a meeting on first call, notice for a meeting on second call (which must be held within thirty days of the date for which the first meeting was called), must be given at least eight days before the date of the second meeting. The by-laws may authorize that both meetings (on first and on second call) be convened by means of the same notice. In this latter case, if the meeting is convened for the same day, it must be held with an interval of not less than one hour between each meeting.

[69] The minutes of all shareholders' meetings, as well as board resolutions, must be transcribed in the official books held by the SA for that purpose. In some cases copies of the minutes have to be filed with the PRC (i.e., minutes of the board and shareholders' meetings related to the approval of annual financial statements and appointment of directors of the SA).

Shareholders' Liability

[70] Shareholders of SAs are only liable for the obligations incurred by the company to the extent of the shareholders' capital commitments or contributions because the company is a legal entity independent from its shareholders. The shareholders are liable only for the capital they have agreed to contribute to the corporation. Each shareholder is liable only for their own pending capital contribution.

[71] Shareholders who have fully paid shares are generally not liable for the company's obligations beyond their capital contributions. Shareholders with partly paid shares are required to pay up any outstanding balance on their shares within a maximum period of two years from the date of subscription.

[72] Any shareholder with interests in conflict with those of the company has a duty to abstain from voting on any matter that relates to such conflict. If the shareholder does not observe this provision, it will be liable for resulting damages from a final resolution of the matter in conflict, if, without the shareholder's vote, the majority vote necessary to adopt such resolution would not have been obtained.

[73] Further, all shareholders who vote in favour of a resolution that is subsequently declared void may be jointly and severally liable, without limitation, for any consequences resulting therefrom.

[74] The CL provides that shareholders or those effectively exercising control over a company who cause damage to the company are jointly liable for such damages and cannot set off such damages against profits that their action may have produced in connection with other transactions of the company. The shareholders or those exercising control that use funds or assets of the company in a transaction for their own benefit must contribute any profits to the company and must bear the losses themselves.

[75] In addition, the bankruptcy of a company can be extended to a controlling shareholder in certain cases, for example, if a shareholder disposes of assets of the company as if they were the shareholder's own, thereby defrauding the company's creditors. A similar result would ensue if any controlling person steered the company's interest in the direction of the controlling shareholder's interest or the economic group to which he or she is a party.

Supervision

[76] Shareholders may at their annual meeting elect one or more statutory supervisors (*síndicos*). Statutory supervisors must be Argentine residents and must be attorneys or accountants duly registered to practice, or a corporation or partnership exclusively formed by such professionals. They may serve for a period not exceeding three fiscal years, with possible re-election. Their functions are to supervise the administration of the company, attend all board and shareholders' meetings and, in general, control the legality of the corporation's decisions. In broad terms, they protect the rights of shareholders and verify that the company abides by the law and its by-laws.

[77] The appointment of statutory supervisors is, in principle, not mandatory. If the company dispenses with the appointment of statutory supervisors, at least one alternate director must be designated.

[78] However, an SA with capital exceeding the sum of ARS10 m must appoint at least one statutory supervisor and one alternate statutory supervisor. Furthermore, if, the company, *inter alia,* publicly offers its shares, operates public concessions or services, performs capitalization or savings operations or operations which in general solicit funds from the public, the law requires that a supervisory committee (*comisión fiscalizadora*) comprised of at least three statutory supervisors be appointed.

Dividends

[79] Dividends may be lawfully declared and paid to shareholders only out of the company's earned and liquid net profits arising from a year-end audited balance sheet duly approved by the annual shareholders' meeting.

[80] No profits may be distributed until prior losses are covered. An SA must set aside at least 5% of its annual net profits for the purposes of creating a reserve fund until the fund reaches 20% of the authorized capital.

[81] Interim dividends may be declared and paid in certain cases. For example, listed companies and companies with capital exceeding the sum of ARS10 m may pay interim dividends.

[82] Directors and statutory supervisors are subject to unlimited joint and several liabilities, for any unauthorized dividend distribution.

[83] Law No. 27,430 sets forth that the SA is subject to a tax rate of 30% for 2018 and 2019, which is reduced to 25% for the following years.

Dividends or profits paid by Argentine companies to individuals and undivided estates residents in Argentina are taxed at the rate of 7% if the income obtained by the SA was subject to the 30% rate and 7% if the income obtained by the SA was subject to a 25% tax.

It will also be applicable for dividends and profits that will be paid to foreign beneficiaries by way of withholdings made by the Argentine entity at the moment of payment. The Income Tax Law (ITL) establishes a presumption of dividend distribution in the case of certain transactions between the SA and its shareholders.

Sociedad Anónima Unipersonal

Shareholders: Incorporation

[84] Following the international trends, the CL was amended to include SAUs as one of the types of business organization that can be adopted. An SAU is formed with a single shareholder that can be either a legal entity or an individual. There are no nationality or residence requirements, foreign individuals (whether resident in Argentina or not) or non-Argentine companies may hold up to 100% of the share capital.

[85] The CL imposes on SAU the incorporation requirements of SA, including further requisites as follows: (i) SAU cannot incorporate another SAU; (ii) SAU share capital shall be fully subscribed and paid up upon incorporation; and (iii) SAU corporate name shall include the expression '*sociedad anónima unipersonal*', its abbreviation or the acronym 'S.A.U'.

[86] The general stipulations that rule the SA as explained above, such as shares, transfer of shares, registration with the PRC, management, directors liability, shareholders' meetings, shareholders' liability and dividends, may apply to SAU, with exceptions to be further explained herein.

Capital

[87] The minimum capital required is ARS100 000. Unlike the SAs, the share capital of SAUs must be fully subscribed and paid in at the time of incorporation. In the event of a capital increase, the capital contribution shall also be fully subscribed and paid in at the time of subscription of the shares.

Permanent Government Supervision

[88] SAUs are subject to permanent government control provided in Article 299 of the CL. In this respect, SAUs must comply with the filings applicable to companies subject to permanent government control required by the PRC of the jurisdiction where the company has its registered domicile. Among others, an SAU must give official notice to the PRC of its annual ordinary shareholders' meeting prior to holding any such meeting.

Management: Board of Directors

[89] The SAU must appoint a board of directors of a minimum of three directors. The remaining general dispositions of the board of directors of the SA apply.

Supervision

[90] The SAU must appoint a supervisory committee (*comisión fiscalizadora*) comprised of at least three regular and three alternate statutory supervisors, being the committee always comprised by members in odd numbers. As explained above, statutory supervisors must be Argentine residents and must be attorneys or accountants duly registered to practice, or a corporation or partnership exclusively formed by such professionals.

Sociedad de Responsabilidad Limitada

Partners: Capital

[91] SRLs are limited liability companies that may be formed with a minimum of two and a maximum of fifty partners or quota holders. Partners may be either individuals or corporate legal entities.

[92] Foreign corporate entities have been admitted as partners of SRLs provided that they are empowered to participate in such partnerships according to the laws of their jurisdiction of incorporation. Since there are no nationality or residence requirements, foreign individuals (whether resident in Argentina or not) or non-Argentine companies may hold up to 100% of the capital.

[93] Where the quota holders of an SRL are Argentine companies, the CL limits a domestic company's participation in other companies from being greater than 100% of its voluntary reserves and 50% of its capital and the legal reserves, if its purpose is not exclusively that of a holding company or financial entity.

[94] There is no minimum capital required to set up an SRL. The capital is divided into quotas (*cuotas*), which are interests in the capital of the company, and which must be expressed in Argentine currency. Quotas must be of equal par value ARS10 or its multiples and entitle the holder to one vote each.

[95] While the capital of an SRL must be fully subscribed upon incorporation, only 25% needs to be paid in at the time of subscription of the quotas and the balance within the following two years. Contributions of real estate, equipment or other non-monetary assets must be made in full upon subscription.

Quotas: Transferability – Rights

[96] Quotas are not represented physically by certificates, so quota holdings are reflected in the by-laws of the company and, thereafter, from the subsequent quota transfer documents, duly registered with the PRC.

[97] SRLs cannot be listed on an official stock exchange.

[98] Transfers of quotas between the partners are not restricted by law but may be restricted under the by-laws. Quotas may be transferred to third parties but existing partners may oppose the incorporation of such third parties to the company if they provide 'just cause' as defined by law. The transfer of quotas is valid vis-à-vis third parties as from its registration with the PRC.

[99] SRLs may provide for options or rights of first refusal either in a quotaholders' agreement or in the provisions of its by-laws, as an effective means to secure a close rein over the transfer of ownership. A provision in the by-laws is always more effective than the agreement executed among the quota holders since the latter is only binding with respect to the contracting parties.

Registration, Annual Fees and Corporate Books

[100] SRLs must be registered with the PRC of the jurisdiction of incorporation (i.e., the City of Buenos Aires or any of the provinces). In the City of Buenos Aires, an SRL registered with the PRC does not pay annual fees to the PRC.

[101] The following resolutions must be registered with the PRC: (i) the transfer and pledge of quotas; (ii) the appointment, removal or resignation of managers; (iii) changes of legal domicile (registered office); (v) any modification to the by-laws; (vi) any capital increase; and (vii) any corporate reorganization.

[102] Annual financial statements are not required to be filed with the PRC unless the SRL's capital exceeds ARS10 m.

[103] Foreign entities that are partners of a local company must register their by-laws, any amendments thereof and other incorporation documents with the PRC.

[104] SRLs must keep the following corporate books: 'management minute book' and 'partners' meetings minute book' (or a single 'minutes book' for both management and shareholders' meeting minutes). In addition, accounting books must be kept.

Management

[105] The partners may appoint one or more managers to manage and represent the company. The managers may be appointed for either a determinate or indeterminate period, as established in the by-laws or when appointed. Alternate managers may be appointed to replace regular managers in case of a vacancy. The managers represent the company, either individually or jointly as set forth in the by-laws.

[106] The majority of the managers must be Argentine residents, regardless of their nationality. Managers need not be partners themselves.

Managers' Liability

[107] Managers of an SRL are subject to a standard of loyalty and diligence; noncompliance with this standard gives rise to unlimited, joint and several liability for damages arising therefrom.

[108] Managers of a company have the duty: (a) to reveal any conflict of interest to the partners, the other managers (in case of plural management) and the statutory supervisor/s if appointed; and (b) to refrain from competing with the company unless it is expressly allowed by the partners by unanimous decision.

[109] Managers are individually or severally liable according to the organization of the management. In the case of plural management, different liabilities can be attributed to each of the managers, depending on their individual acts.

Partners' Meetings

[110] The by-laws normally contain the rules for adopting resolutions. However, if the by-laws do not set forth specific rules, resolutions may be passed in writing without the need for holding a meeting.

[111] Resolutions concerning either amendments to the by-laws or the appointment or removal of managers or statutory supervisors must be passed by the majority as established in the by-laws, which must consist of at least the affirmative vote of partners who represent over 50% of the company's capital. If the by-laws are silent on what constitutes a majority, the affirmative vote of the partners that represent over 75% of the company's capital is required. If one partner represents the majority vote, another partner's vote is also required.

[112] Resolutions concerning issues other than amendments to the by-laws, or the appointment or removal of managers or statutory supervisors, must be passed by the affirmative vote of the partners who represent over 50% of the capital participating in such resolution or present in such meeting unless the by-laws provide for a higher majority.

[113] If the company's capital exceeds the sum of ARS10 m, the partners must hold an annual meeting to consider the financial accounts of the previous year, which must be called within four months following the fiscal year-end. Such meetings are validly held on first call with the presence of partners representing the majority of quotas of the company's capital; on second call with the presence of any partners regardless of the number of quotas they represent. In both cases, resolutions must be passed by the affirmative vote of the absolute majority of votes present.

[114] If a quorum is not available in a meeting on first call, a notice for a meeting on second call (which must be held within thirty days of the date for which the first meeting was called) must be given at least eight days before the date of the second meeting. The by-laws may authorize that both meetings (on first and on second call) are convened by means of the same notice. In this latter case, if the meeting is convened for the same day, it must be held with an interval of not less than one hour between each meeting. All partners' resolutions must be transcribed into a minute book and signed.

Partners' Liability

[115] Partners enjoy limited liability up to the capital subscribed in the SRL. However, each quota holder guarantees vis-à-vis third parties, jointly and severally, and without limit: (i) all pending capital contributions, whether pertaining to the holder or not, and whether monetary or non-monetary; and (ii) the overvaluation of non-monetary contributions, whether its own or not.

[116] In the event of a transfer of quotas, the guarantee of the assignor continues to apply to corporate liabilities assumed up to the time of the transfer registration. The purchaser guarantees unlimitedly the capital contributions jointly and severally, and without limitation, with no distinction as to commitments before or after the date of the registration. The assignor who has not paid in full his or her quotas is liable severally and jointly with the assignee for the amount still to be paid in. The company may not demand payment from the assignee without first pursuing the assignor in arrears.

[117] Any partner with interests in conflict with those of the company has a duty to abstain from voting on any matter that relates to such conflict. If that partner does not observe this provision, the partner will be liable for any resulting damages from a final resolution of the matter in conflict, if the majority vote necessary to adopt such resolution would not have been obtained without the partner's vote.

[118] Furthermore, all partners that vote in favour of a resolution that is subsequently declared void may *be jointly liable, without limit, for any consequences resulting therefrom.*

Controllership

[119] An SRL whose capital exceeds the sum of ARS10 m must appoint at least one regular and one alternate statutory supervisor (*síndico*). Statutory supervisors must be Argentine residents and must be attorneys or accountants duly registered to practice, or a corporation or partnership exclusively formed by such professionals. They may serve for a period not exceeding three fiscal years, with possible re-election. Their functions are to supervise the administration of the company, attend managers and partners' meetings and, in general, control the legality of the company's decisions. In broad terms, they protect the rights of partners and verify that the company abides by the law and its by-laws.

[120] Statutory supervisors are subject to unlimited joint and several liability for not observing the obligations imposed on them by law or the by-laws. They can also be held jointly and severally liable for the managers' acts or omissions as a consequence of their failure to control the managers' acts.

Sociedades por Acciones Simplificadas

Shareholders

[121] One or more corporate entities or individuals as shareholders. The limited liability is subject to the integration of the shares. Shareholder meetings may be held electronically and outside the company's premises.

Incorporation

[122] Registration must be completed within twenty-four hours from the next business day after the filing, as long as the filings are made electronically with a standard form. The incorporation, or any amendments, may be made by public deed, a duly legalized private instrument or electronically with a digital signature. This procedure includes digital notices for PRC observations. In case the draft by-laws approved by the PRC are not adopted, the registration may take at least twenty days.

[123] An SAS can obtain a tax ID within twenty-four hours of being filed with the Argentine Tax Authority (the 'AFIP' after its acronym in Spanish), and there is no need to provide evidence of domicile at the beginning of the filing.

Board of Directors

[124] The simplified corporation must have at least one effective and one alternate director, in the case of no statutory supervisors. These posts may be appointed for certain or uncertain terms. With regards to the effective directors, at least one must have residency in Argentina. This new type of entity also allows meetings of the board of directors to be held electronically and outside the company's premises.

Limitations

[125] An SAS cannot incorporate or participate in another SAS. An SAS cannot be controlled by or connected in more than 30% of its corporate capital with a company in the terms of 299 CL.

Initial Capital

[126] At first, corporate capital cannot be less than two times the minimum salary. Capital is divided into shares with singular or plural vote. Capital integration is based on the terms and conditions of the by-laws.

Capital Increase

[127] Up to 50% of the registered capital does not need to be registered. Issuance of shares with different primes is allowed.

Contributions

[128] The value of in-kind contributions may be unanimously set by the shareholders, or by market value as a default. Irrevocable contributions may maintain such nature for twenty-four months.

Shares Assignment

[129] The assignment of shares will be done according to the by-laws and may require shareholder approval. If it is not determined in the by-laws, any assignment must be notified to the company and registered within the Shares Registry Book to be effective against third parties. Limitations may be included in the by-laws for a prohibition of the assignment of shares of up to ten years.

Transformation

[130] All companies incorporated based on CL may be transformed into SAS.

Digital Records

[131] SAS companies must have a digital minute book as well as books for share registry, logs, inventory and the balance sheet. The company's by-laws, its amendments and power of attorneys may be granted through the digital notarial protocol.

Registration of Foreign Legal Entities as Shareholders or Partners of Local Companies

[132] If a foreign company wishes to be a shareholder or partner in a local company, it must first register its by-laws and other qualifying documents with the PRC and appoint an attorney-in-fact in Argentina. Also, accounting documents and/or certificates must be filed at the time of registering the foreign corporate entity with the PRC.

Foreign Exchange Regulations

[133] As a result of Argentina's financial crisis of 2001/2002, new foreign exchange controls, cross-border transfer restrictions, and the mandatory repatriation of export and services proceeds were reinstated beginning 2002. During the year 2002, the Argentine Central Bank enacted several foreign exchange regulations addressed to restrict most cross-border capital, interest, profit and dividend transfers, which from then on needed the Argentine Central Bank's prior authorization. Nevertheless, the original restrictions have been progressively loosened by the Argentine Central Bank.

[134] There are currently no issues in moving currency from Argentina. Although foreign exchange controls in Argentina remain in place, it is worth mentioning that since the current administration took over (i.e., 10 December 2015), the Argentine Central Bank (the 'Central Bank') has been revising and issuing many foreign exchange and trade rules relaxing foreign exchange restrictions—especially those related to the outflows of funds.

[135] As of today, the Central Bank has abrogated all foreign exchange restrictions, and the only foreign exchange regulations which remain in place refer to operational aspects and the applicable information regimes. As a general rule, all transfers of foreign currency to and from Argentina must be made through the Argentine Foreign Exchange Market (the 'FX Market') and are subject to compliance with certain formal requirements set forth in the regulations that are periodically issued by the Central Bank as the regulatory authority in charge of administering the FX Market. All transactions made through the FX Market are registered under a specific code (*código de concepto*) for statistical purposes only.

[136] Currently, both Argentine and non-Argentine residents can freely access the FX Market. Access to the FX Market is done at the market exchange rate. The exchange rate is determined by the relevant counterparties, but the Central Bank has the power to intervene by buying and selling foreign currency for its own account, a practice in which it engages on a regular basis.

[137] As of 31 December 2017, the so-called Survey on issuance of notes and other obligations of the private financial and non-financial sectors set forth by Communique 'A' 3602 and the so-called Survey on direct investments held abroad and locally set forth by Communique 'A' 4237, have been replaced by Communique 'A' 6401 for the 'Survey of External Assets and Liabilities', which unifies all reporting obligations. Such survey is made solely for statistical purposes and non-compliance does not impede access to the FX Market.

Regulated Activities

[138] Financial institutions, insurance companies, companies authorized to publicly offer their securities, utilities and companies involved in telecommunications, media and airline activities, are subject to regulation, inspection and supervision by the relevant government agencies.

[139] Pursuant to Financial Entities Law No. 21,526, the Argentine Central Bank is responsible for the regulation, inspection and supervision of financial institutions. In particular, it has discretionary power to authorize the operation, merger and transfer of the banking business of financial institutions.

[140] Companies that publicly offer securities are subject to CNV Rules. Two or more public companies wishing to merge, whether by setting up a new company or as an absorbing or absorbed company must apply for approval of the merger and early dissolution by submitting a prospectus to the CNV, at least thirty days prior to the date the merger is to be considered. If the absorbing company is subject to CNV regulations and the absorbed company is regulated by another agency, the absorbing company must request the CNV's approval for the merger. The absorbed company must request its supervisory agency for administrative approval of its dissolution. Moreover, if the absorbing company is regulated by another agency, and the absorbed company is regulated by the CNV regulations, the absorbing company must request its supervising agency's approval for the merger, and the absorbed company must request CNV's approval of its dissolution.

[141] Pursuant to Law No. 26,425, which set the Integrated Retirement Pension System (*'Sistema Integrado de Jubilaciones de Pensiones'* or *SIJP*), Pension Fund Managers (*'Administradoras de Fondos de Jubilaciones y Pensiones'*, or *AFJP*) ceased to administer the pension funds of those workers who had chosen the capitalization system, and all the pension funds are currently managed by the National Social Security Administration (*'Administración Nacional de la Seguridad Social'* or *ANSES*). Most Pension Fund Managers were dissolved.

[142] Telecommunications companies (currently named Communications and Information Technologies Services' providers – *TIC Services*-) are regulated by Digital Argentina Law No. 27,078 and Emergency Decree No. 267/2015 and are subject to the supervision and control of the National Communications Entity (*'Enacom'*), an autarchic and decentralized entity under the jurisdiction of the Argentine Communications Ministry. All transfers of TIC Services licenses or any transaction that imply a direct or indirect change in controlling shareholdings of TIC Services' licensors are subject to the subsequent approval of the Enacom. The Enacom approval may be granted expressly or by deemed approval if the Enacom does not make any official observation within 90 days. The implementation of any transfers of TIC Services licenses or shares without the corresponding express or deemed approval of the Enacom is subject to revocation by the Enacom. Further, any transfer or lease of radio-spectrum frequencies must be previously approved by the Enacom. Telecommunications regulations impose certain restrictions as regards the awarding of licenses and the quantity of spectrum to be granted to a person or entity that may impact on a merger or acquisition.

Capital Market Regulations

[143] On 27 December 2012 the new Securities Law No. 26,831 was enacted, modifying the public offer regime set forth by Law No. 17,811, as amended (*Securities Law*). The regulation of the Securities Law was approved in August 2013 by Decree No. 1,023/2013 and in September 2013 the CNV completed the analysis of the new framework through Resolution No. 622/2013, as amended. On 9 May 2018 the Securities Law was amended by Law No. 27,440 of Productive Financing. The CNV is responsible for the enforcement of the Securities Law and its regulations and is empowered to issue further regulations.

[144] Under the Securities Law, transactions with securities may be carried out through public offerings or private offerings. The Securities Law only applies to 'public offerings' in Argentina and not to private offerings.

[145] Although the Securities Law was intended as a thorough change to the public offering regime established by Law No. 17,811, it did not introduce substantial changes in what it is a 'public offering' of securities. The definition of 'public offering' provided by the Securities Law is still very broad and provides no 'safe-harbours' or bright-line tests that may be used to determine if an offering is a 'public offering' that requires registration with the CNV or a private offering that does not. A private offering still has to be defined by exclusion, as an offering that does not fall within the 'public offering' definition provided by the Securities Law. In any event, each case needs to be analysed applying common sense to determine if a particular action may be considered a public offering. Additionally, the Securities Law does not have extraterritorial effects; therefore, public offerings carried out abroad are not subject to the Securities Law or CNV supervision.

[146] A 'public offer' is an invitation, made by an issuer or by individuals or companies engaged fully or partially in the trading of securities, to the general public, or certain sectors or groups thereof, through personal offers, newspaper advertisements, radio or television broadcasts, films, billboards, electronic means such as e-mails and social networks, signs, programmes, circulars, printed notices or by any other means, to enter into any transaction involving securities. The term 'transaction' is construed by the Securities Law in the broadest sense, including the initial issue and placement of securities (initial offer) as well as the subsequent purchase and/or sale thereof (secondary market).

[147] In order to be engaged in a public offering of securities, issuers, registered agents authorized by the CNV, and other entities involved in the public offer must be registered with the CNV. The Securities Law provides that only securities that have identical rights within each class may be publicly offered. CNV approval of the public offering means only that there was compliance with the regulations applicable to the offer and does not provide any assurance with respect to the subsequent performance of the particular security as an investment. The approval of a particular issue does not apply to subsequent issues of the same or another type of securities by an issuer; however, once that issuer has been authorized to make a public offering of securities, a simpler and more accelerated procedure is available for subsequent issues.

[148] Issuers who have received authorization must continue to observe certain reporting requirements and are subject to the supervision of the CNV as long as they are authorized to offer their securities publicly, regardless whether they have any public security outstanding on not.

[149] The Securities Law eliminates the markets' self-regulation. It expressly provides that stock exchanges and securities markets can no longer impose as a requirement for membership to be a shareholder of the market. It also establishes that securities markets must be organized as public companies, excluding other types of corporations or civil associations.

[150] Moreover, the CNV is now empowered to directly authorize, revoke, regulate and supervise the securities markets, their participants. Accordingly, the CNV is entitled to determine the requirements that the markets and their participants must have in order to be authorized as such.

[151] The Securities Law created several types of licenses in order to engage in the public offering of securities. Under prior Law No. 17,811, there was a single license for all broker-dealer activities. The Securities Law, however, includes at least five licenses that are related to broker-dealer activities: broker-dealer license, an underwriter license, a clearing member license, a global investment advisor license and capital market advisor license.

[152] The public offer of authorized securities may take place either at a *Bolsas y Mercados Argentinos* (stock market) or in the *Mercado Abierto* (open or over-the-counter market (MAE)).

[153] There are six stock markets in Argentina of which by far the most important is the *Bolsas y Mercados Argentinos S.A.* (BYMA).

[154] Stock markets are affiliated to exchanges. There are many stock exchanges in Argentina. The most important stock exchange is the *Bolsa de Comercio de Buenos Aires* that was absorbed by BYMA

[155] Exchanges, in conjunction with the CNV, act as regulating authorities with respect to their affiliated stock markets. In this function, exchanges provide their own internal rules which, among other things, establish the conditions for listing securities, admitting brokers, conducting trade and controlling the accuracy of any information which is required to be reported in connection therewith. Such internal rules must be approved by the CNV. Likewise, the fees charged by exchanges for admittance to listing and other services must be approved by the CNV. Exchanges must adapt their internal rules to the Securities Law and the CNV's new regulations pursuant Resolution No. 622/2013.

[156] As noted above, besides stock markets, securities may be publicly offered on the open market. Only the issuers of authorized securities and individuals and entities authorized by and registered at the CNV (open market agents) may conduct activity in this market.

[157] Ancillary institutions that assist trading are the *Cajas de Valores* (clearinghouses). These are private organizations that act as clearinghouses for securities transactions.

[158] There are currently several risk rating agencies, including Standard & Poor's, Moody's and Fix Ratings, which are registered with the CNV.

[159] Investors in the securities market consist of individuals, companies, financial trusts, and institutional investors such as investment funds, financial entities and the Argentine Social Security Administration.

[160] There are no particular limitations applicable to the negotiation of securities by individuals or companies. Investment funds have limitations imposed on them by regulatory laws and rules.

[161] The Buenos Aires Stock Exchange has three different trading systems: the traditional auction system, a computer-assisted trading system (*Sistema Integrado de Negociacion Asistida por Computador*, SINAC) and a continuous electronic market which is similar to, but separate from, the MAE. Equities, options and futures are traded exclusively on the Buenos Aires Stock Exchange, and Argentine government and corporate debt securities may be traded either on the Buenos Aires Stock Exchange or on the MAE. Commodity options and futures are traded in special markets which are not as yet highly developed.

[162] The clearing of transactions on the Buenos Aires Stock Exchange is carried out through an organization that was absorbed by BYMA, the *Caja de Valores S.A.*, the Argentine clearing agency that provides central depository facilities for securities and that may act as a transfer and paying agent. Settlement is carried out through the BYMA. Over-the-counter transactions are cleared and settled by their respective parties, and the participants (known as depositors) may deposit the traded securities with the *Caja de Valores S.A.*, which then holds them on behalf of their principals or beneficial owners (*comitentes*).

[163] As a general rule, the Securities Law and the regulations of the CNV provide that any kind of security may be issued and publicly offered, provided that such securities are issued in series and that the securities within each series have the same characteristics.

[164] The regulations of the CNV set out specific procedures regarding the registration of debt securities, asset-backed securities, pooled funds or investment funds, direct investment funds and money market funds.

[165] Corporate debt securities to be offered to the public may be rated by one or two rating agencies, but the rating is no longer a mandatory requirement to offer such securities in the market. In addition, issuers may request that the rating agencies rate their equity securities. Rating agencies must be approved and authorized by the CNV.

[166] Companies incorporated in foreign countries may offer their securities to the public pursuant to the same conditions and requirements as those applicable to Argentine issuers or, alternatively, through Argentine depositary receipts (*Certificados de Depósito Argentinos*, CEDEARS) representing their securities issued by local entities (either through sponsored or non-sponsored programmes or through securities certificates, '*Certificados de Valores*' or *CEVA*) in accordance with specific CNV requirements. The CNV may establish less onerous requirements for companies that have securities listed in countries that have cooperation agreements with Argentina or, in the absence of such agreements, where the CNV determines that existing regulations afford reasonable protection to domestic investors and ensure adequate disclosure of information.

Insider Trading

[167] The Securities Law and regulations of the CNV forbid the use of privileged information for the benefit of the persons who have access to such information or for the benefit of third parties. The CNV has issued resolutions in order to prevent the misappropriation of non-public information and to guarantee fair dealing in the securities market. These resolutions require that the CNV be informed of any facts that may affect the placement and/or trading of securities. In addition, it imposes a duty on certain persons to keep secret all relevant information that has not been publicly disclosed and that may have an impact on the placement and/or trading of securities. Furthermore, the regulations prohibit the use of privileged information for the benefit of the persons who have access to such information or for the benefit of third parties and to trade with the securities involved until such relevant information is publicly disclosed by the persons in charge to do so.

[168] The Securities Law also requires that controlling shareholders, directors, managers, statutory supervisors, members of the supervisory committee and any other person who by reason of their position, activity or relationship obtains information, take all the measures necessary to prevent their subordinates or third parties from gaining access to such privileged information.

[169] Pursuant to the Securities Law, if insider trading activities are identified, the issuer or the shareholders are entitled to recovery proceedings in connection with the use of privileged information by insiders ('short swing profits'). Besides, these activities are subject to the following sanctions, which may be imposed by the CNV: (a) Written warning, which may be accompanied by the publication of the relevant resolution in the Official Gazette and two national newspapers. (b) Fines of up to ARS100 000 000, which may be raised up to five times the benefit obtained by the insider if it was higher. (c) Disqualification for up to five years to act as directors, administrators, members of the supervisory board, accountants or external auditors or managers of any entity subject to the supervision of the CNV. (d) Cancellation of up to two years of the authorization to make public offering. (e) Prohibition to make public offering of securities or to act in the sphere of the public offering.

Most Common Types of Transactions

[170] The ownership of a business enterprise may be transferred by means of the acquisition of the equity or share capital of the target company or the purchase of the business assets from the target company as a going concern, or by way of a merger. Assets can be purchased for cash or exchanged for shares. Share transactions can also result in a cash or share consideration.

[171] M&A activity is regulated by the Civil and Commercial Code, and supplementary legislation. The Civil and Commercial Code entered into effect on 1 August 2015 providing a thorough amendment of the current legal framework and unification of the former Argentine Civil and Commercial Codes. Because of the extension of the reform and the lack of case law under this Civil and Commercial Code, its impact is continuously being assessed and is expected to evolve over time.

Mergers are specially provided for in the CL. Acquisitions are not subject to specific legislation; their regulation stems from the general rules applicable to corporations and partnerships, commercial contracts and securities. Share purchase agreements are subject to the applicable provisions of the Civil and Commercial Code, while asset transfer agreements are regulated by Federal Law No. 11,867

(Bulk Transfer Law), which sets forth a procedure mainly aimed at protecting the seller's creditors.

[172] M&A transactions generally fall within the scope of commercial law, with the exception of certain aspects (tax, labour, etc.) that are contemplated in other branches of law. M&A activity involving state-owned companies is further regulated by administrative law.

[173] In general, off-exchange, private merger and acquisition transactions are not legally subject to prior substantive scrutiny by governmental, judicial or other bodies, except where they fall within the scope of Antitrust Law or involve specific industries.

[174] Should the company's activity be a regulated activity, additional requirements and regulations may be applicable. Financial institutions, insurance companies, companies authorized to offer their securities publicly, utilities and companies involved in telecommunications are subject to regulation, inspection and supervision by the relevant government agencies as to the transfer of their shares.

[175] Take-over bids of companies that are authorized to publicly offer their shares are governed by the Securities Law and further specific regulations of the CNV. These regulations provide for requirements to be fulfilled in both voluntary and compulsory tender offers. The stock exchanges have not enacted express rules governing take-over bids. However, in the case of listed companies, any disclosure of information regarding any take-over bid which is submitted to the CNV must also be submitted and filed with the stock exchange where the relevant company is listed.

[176] CNV Rules must be complied with by any person who intends to obtain control of a company that makes a public offering of its shares for the purpose of a take-over bid. The Securities Law and CNV Rules apply both to purchase offers and to share exchange offers.

[177] Take-over bids of private companies are not expressly governed by the CL or any specific law. General rules of the CL apply to take-over bids, but such rules do not specifically contemplate tender offers. General rules established in the Civil and Commercial Code regarding the execution of contracts may also be applicable (e.g., promise of contract, revocability of the offer). In several cases, the PRC has followed the legal framework applied to listed companies, and thus certain CNV Rules, such as those regarding fair price, should also be considered.

Mergers

Types of Merger

[178] Mergers are governed by the CL. The CL provides for *consolidations*, where two or more companies transfer their assets and liabilities to a new company which, as consideration, issues shares to the shareholders of the merged companies which are then dissolved. The CL also provides for *mergers*, where one or more companies transfer their assets and liabilities to an existing company that, as consideration, issues shares to the shareholders of the absorbed company/companies, which are then dissolved.

Preliminary Merger Agreement

[179] The rules on mergers require that a preliminary merger agreement be entered into between all the companies party to the merger. This preliminary merger agreement must contain:

(i) The reasons for the merger.
(ii) Special merger balance sheets for each company, including an auditor's report. If the company has a statutory supervisor (*síndico*), he or she must also prepare a report. All financial related documents must be prepared using identical valuation criteria.
(iii) The equity exchange ratio, indicating the relevant equity (whether quotas or shares) that the merging companies' partners or shareholders will receive in the new or surviving company.
(iv) Any management agreements and/or guarantees given to ensure regular conduction of business until the merger is duly registered with the PRC.

[180] The preliminary merger agreement and the special merger balance sheets must be approved by the appropriate corporate body (i.e., boards of directors or managers) and by shareholders or partners of the merging companies.

Creditors' Rights

[181] In order to protect creditors' rights, a notice of the mergers must be published in the Official Gazette in each company's jurisdiction and in a newspaper of nationwide circulation. Creditors opposing the transaction must file an objection within fifteen days of the publication of all the relevant notices. The filing of an objection does not prevent the merger, but execution of the final agreement will be suspended for an additional period of twenty days after the initial fifteen-day period has expired. This is to allow opposing creditors who are not paid off or whose debts are not duly secured by the companies involved in the transaction, to obtain judicial liens. If creditors are not sufficiently secured or paid, a judicial claim may be filed by the creditor, resorting to the more expeditious summary proceeding.

Final Merger Agreement

[182] Once the fifteen-day period for objection by creditors has elapsed and no objection has been filed, or once creditors who have opposed have been paid out or secured, the final merger agreement may be executed. It must contain:

(i) Each merging company's resolution approving the merger.

(ii) A list of the partners or shareholders who have exercised their appraisal right and the portion of capital they represent in each company.
(iii) A list of opposing creditors whose credits have been secured and who have obtained judicial liens; in both cases, descriptions of the claims and any preliminary injunctions obtained must be included; a list of creditors who have been paid, together with a brief report on their impact on the special merger balance sheets.
(iv) The special merger balance sheets and a consolidated balance sheet of the merging companies.

Appraisal Rights

[183] Whenever shareholders of a company approve a merger in which their company is not the surviving company, any shareholder who voted against such action or did not attend the meeting at which such action was approved may withdraw from the company and receive the value of its shares, determined on the basis of the company's most recent audited balance sheet (i.e., the merger balance sheet).

[184] Appraisal rights must be exercised within five days following the adjournment of the meeting at which the resolution was adopted in the event the dissenting shareholder voted against such resolution or within fifteen days following such adjournment if the dissenting shareholder did not attend such meeting. The exercise of appraisal rights will entail modifications to the merger balance sheet and may also alter exchange ratios.

Registration

[185] The law requires that the final merger agreement be registered with the PRC. If the final merger agreements, by-laws of the new company, capital increase or modification of the by-laws of the surviving company are not registered, the merger will have no legal effect vis-à-vis third parties.

[186] Until the final merger agreement is registered with the PRC, the companies involved in the merger must comply with their obligations of preparing and approving the annual financial statements and filing them with the PRC, and of payment of annual fees to the PRC. The filing of annual financial statements is not applicable to an SRL unless its capital exceeds ARS10 m.

[187] Since a merger will cause the dissolution of one or more companies, which cease to exist as legal entities, post-merger notices of the completed transaction should be given to other interested third parties.

Tax Aspects

[188] To encourage business reorganizations, Argentine tax law provides that, in principle, such mergers shall not give rise to any tax liability, provided that specific conditions are satisfied. Further details are given under 'Taxation' below.

Public Companies

[189] In the event of merger of public companies, publication requirements under both the CL and CNV Rules must be observed. The CL requires publication for three days in the Official Gazette of the jurisdiction of each merging company. Furthermore, CNV Rules require the publication of the prospectus submitted to the CNV in a widely circulated newspaper. If such companies list their securities on the Buenos Aires Stock Exchange or any other stock exchange, the publication shall be fulfilled by publishing the prospectus in the bulletin of the relevant exchange.

Spin-Offs

[190] Argentine law defines a spin-off as an operation by which a company:

(a) separates part of its assets and liabilities from its existing assets and liabilities and either:
  (i) creates (together with another company) a new company to which these assets or liabilities are transferred; or
  (ii) merges such assets and liabilities into one or more existing companies (in which latter case the rules applicable to mergers will apply);
(b) separates part of its assets and liabilities from its existing assets and liabilities and creates one or more companies to which these assets and liabilities are transferred;
(c) creates new companies into which all of its assets and liabilities are transferred.

The companies to which assets and liabilities have been transferred then issue shares to the shareholders of the company that has spun-off the assets and liabilities.

Procedure

[191] As in the case of mergers, the procedure for spin-offs requires that the relevant company approve the operation, the spin-off balance sheets, the issue and distribution of shares and the relevant amendments to the by-laws.

Creditors' Rights

[192] Creditors in spin-offs are entitled to rights similar to those applicable to mergers. Details of the spin-off must also be published in the Official Gazette in the company's jurisdiction and in a newspaper of nationwide circulation.

Appraisal Rights

[193] Similar rules to those applicable to mergers apply.

Registration

[194] The spin-off will be effective vis-à-vis third parties once: the periods provided for appraisal rights, objection by creditors and application for judicial liens have elapsed, without any pending claims; and, the by-laws of the new company and the amendment to the by-laws of the spinning-off company have been executed and registered with the PRC.

Tax Aspects

[195] To encourage business reorganizations, Argentine tax law provides, in principle, that spin-offs shall not give rise to any tax liability, provided that specific conditions are satisfied. Further details are given under 'Taxation' below.

Acquisitions of Shares

General Overview

[196] Strictly speaking, the only way to acquire an Argentine company is to obtain the controlling portion of the target's voting capital. Due to market peculiarities, the pursuit of such an objective in the open market is highly unlikely to succeed. Hostile takeovers are rare and public mergers and acquisitions are in reality almost non-existent. An open market buyer may at best acquire enough stock to obtain a position on the board of directors of the company.

[197] In contrast, private off-exchange mergers and acquisitions are commonplace. They occur among all sizes of companies and involve both local and foreign capital.

[198] Acquisitions of non-listed companies will normally take the form of a private deal, directly negotiated by the offeror and all the shareholders or the controlling shareholders of the target company. A typical acquisition will start either through an investment bank or with the buyer getting in touch with the target's management, which usually includes one or more persons holding a controlling interest, and making a purchase offer. Acquisitions routinely involve meticulous auditing and due diligence procedures, with an emphasis on the target company's tax and labour obligations (taxes, social security, etc.). It is customary to request that special financial statements be prepared at the time of closing. A stock purchase agreement will require careful drafting to encompass all the agreed conditions and will include representation and warranties from the shareholders in the target company in favour of the buyer.

[199] What constitutes a controlling interest in the target company is a question of fact and will depend on its shareholding structure. Control is deemed as the power, either direct or indirect, through equity that gives the necessary votes to govern the corporate will in the corporate bodies and meetings or to exercise a dominant influence.

[200] Notice of acquisitions of shares representing 5% or more of the capital stock of public companies must be given to the CNV, and if listed, to the relevant stock exchange.

Minority Shareholders

[201] With respect to minority shareholders, there is basically no legal action to oppose an acquisition other than that based on the grounds of fraudulent conveyance or breach of directors' fiduciary duties. Beyond this, a minority shareholder might make use of a right of first refusal if provided for in the company's by-laws.

[202] Under the CL, minority shareholders that dissent from certain decisions may withdraw from the corporation and are entitled to reimbursement of the book value of their shares. Such decisions are, *inter alia*: change of corporate form, extension or renewal of the company's duration; transfer of domicile abroad; fundamental change of corporate purpose; total or partial repayment of capital; mergers and divestments (except with regard to the surviving company); and capital increases decided by extraordinary shareholders meetings which involve disbursements by such shareholders.

Shareholders Agreements

[203] Shareholders agreements are only binding on the contracting parties and are, therefore, not enforceable against third parties unless reflected entirely in the company's by-laws. Shareholders agreements whose provisions are not encompassed in the company's by-laws will only give rise to a claim for damages for compensation, and not to 'specific performance' of the obligations, as may be the case in other jurisdictions.

Liabilities

[204] In the case of a share purchase, all liabilities, including hidden and contingent liabilities, are automatically transferred from seller to buyer, unless expressly agreed otherwise. In practice, the parties rely on contractually agreed representations and warranties. Argentine courts have maintained that 'the seller of a shareholding only transfers its rights as a shareholder and does not answer for the existence of hidden debts or other irregularities (with respect to the company's net worth) except where such liability has been expressly agreed upon'.

Acquisitions of Assets

General Overview

[205] Asset transfer agreements are regulated by the Federal Law No. 11,867 (Bulk Transfer Law), which sets forth a procedure mainly aimed at protecting the seller's creditors. In addition, the procedure established by the Bulk Transfer Law also protects the bona fide transferee in case the debts exceed the credits of the going concern.

[206] There is no definition of the term 'going concern' (*fondo de comercio*) in the law, but it establishes that its 'constituting elements' are as follows: fixtures, inventories, company name, clientele, right to the premises, trademarks, patents, industrial and model designs, and all other rights pertaining to commercial, industrial or artistic property. Courts have also considered other elements than those established by the Bulk Transfer Law.

[207] Thus, a sale encompassing these elements would be considered as a transfer of a going concern and would fall within the scope of the Bulk Transfer Law. In this sense, the courts have declared that even if not all of the elements are being transferred, there may still be a transfer of a going concern.

[208] To determine whether a sale of part of the assets of a company constitutes a transfer of a going concern, the following should be taken into consideration:

(i) If the transfer curtails in a substantial manner the basic assets of the seller or its productive capacity.
(ii) If, due to the transfer, the seller is unable to continue its business operations in the same or in a similar way to that carried out prior to said transfer, and in turn, the buyer is left in a position to carry on such operations as the seller did previously.
(iii) The transfer of the company name and of the clientele, as well as a non-compete agreement, are crucial elements to determine the existence of a transfer of business.
(iv) The transfer should not prejudice the seller's creditors.

[209] Court precedents have declared that a transfer of a going concern exists if the buyer acquires the lease, retains the majority of the seller's employees, holds itself out before the public as the seller's successor and forbids the seller to set up a new business within a specific territory during a specific period of time.

Procedure

[210] Under the Bulk Transfer Law, the seller must publish a notice for five days in the Official Gazette, and in the local newspaper of the jurisdiction in which the company subject to the transfer operates, indicating: (i) type and location of the business; (ii) name and domicile of seller and buyer; and (iii) where applicable, the name of the auctioneer and notary public involved in the transaction. In addition, the seller must deliver to the buyer a list with all amounts due and outstanding, giving data relating to creditors, and the characteristics of the credits involved.

[211] The seller's creditors have ten days as of the last day of publication of the notice, to oppose the bulk transfer transaction, by requesting the retention of their credits and the deposit of the sums sufficient to cover them with a special bank account. To such extent, opposing creditors may obtain court orders to attach the deposited amounts within twenty days as from the expiration of the period provided for the oppositions. The deposit of these amounts does not imply payment of the debts of the going concern but it is deemed as a guarantee for the credits in replacement of the assets of the going concern to be transferred.

Registration

[212] The asset transfer agreement may be executed ten days after the last notice is published in case no oppositions are filed, or as soon as the twenty-day term mentioned above has expired. After its execution, it should be filed for its recording with the PRC. Recording of this agreement will take at least six months. The delay in the registration generally derives from the fact that for recording purposes, free-from-indebtedness certificates from the social security and provincial tax authorities should be obtained. The obtaining of these certificates is always a cumbersome and time-consuming process.

[213] If the asset transfer agreement is filed with the PRC within the ten days following its execution, it will maintain its retroactive effect; otherwise, it will not have retroactive effect and, therefore, will not limit the liability of buyer prior to the registration date.

[214] The transfer of a going concern is only effective vis-à-vis third parties as from the date of its registration with the PRC. Until that date, the assets of the going concern shall respond for all of the debts of the seller. In addition, if the proceedings described herein have not been duly observed by seller and buyer (and the auctioneer and the notary public in case they have participated in the transfer of the going concern) shall be jointly and severally liable for the amount of the credits unpaid up to the price of the transfer agreed between the parties.

[215] The purchase price cannot be lower than the credits listed by the seller plus the amounts claimed by unlisted opposing creditors unless all the creditors agree with the purchase price.

Legal Effects

[216] The general principle is that the buyer of the going concern is liable for any responsibilities arising from the going concern, and can only liberate itself through the specified process of notices and after the required waiting periods as described above.

[217] The transfer of the going concern can only be carried out if notices of the contemplated sale are published, and seller's creditors are given the opportunity to obtain a court order attaching the corresponding part of the purchase price which corresponds to their claims.

[218] If this procedure is not followed, the buyer will be jointly liable for the amounts resulting from creditors' claims which remain unpaid, up to a maximum equivalent to the purchase price.

[219] If the parties duly observe the procedure mentioned above, the buyer shall have a 'perfect title' to the seller's going concern, and it will be effective vis-à-vis third parties, except for the tax authorities.

Tax Aspects

[220] As regards national taxes, the Federal Law No. 11,683, as amended (Tax Procedure Law), provides that the buyer of a business is jointly and severally liable with the seller that has not complied with the payment request made by the tax authorities for any unpaid taxes. However, the responsibility of the buyer for the undetermined tax debt will cease: (i) three months after the transfer, if the Tax Board was notified of the transfer at least fifteen working days prior to its effective date and provided the tax authorities do not determine tax debts within the three-month term; or (ii) if the Tax Board admits the solvency of the seller or considers that the security offered by the latter is sufficient.

[221] The tax authorities would, therefore, be allowed to collect unpaid past taxes related to the seller's going concern from the buyer, even if no oppositions have been notified within the legal term mentioned above.

[222] Once the required advance notice is given to the tax authority, the transfer may take place. If three months pass without any action being taken by the authorities, the buyer is free from any liability for any national undetermined tax debt that may be owed by the target company.

[223] It is also advisable to notify provincial tax authorities in those jurisdictions where turnover tax (*impuesto a los ingresos brutos*) is paid.

Labour and Social Security Aspects

[224] In connection with labour obligations, Labour Law No. 20,744, as amended, provides that buyers are jointly and severally liable with sellers with respect to all liabilities arising out of labour relationships before the date of transfer, whereas the buyer becomes solely liable for those arising after the transfer. Buyers and sellers are jointly and severally liable for labour obligations that arise during or as a result of the transfer of the business. The Labour Court of Appeals, in a plenary judgment binding in the City of Buenos Aires, has considered that the buyer of an ongoing concern is also liable for any obligations arising from any labour relationships extinguished before the transfer of the ongoing concern. Labour Law also provides that the employees are entitled to retain the seniority (service) and all seniority rights acquired while working for the transferor.

[225] As regards social security obligations, legal doctrine considers that sellers and buyers are both jointly and severally responsible for them. This construction is based on Labour Law pursuant to which both parties are responsible for all the liabilities arising in connection with the employment relationship. Since the social security obligations arise from such a relationship, both parties are responsible.

[226] The main legal issues under Labour Law are those concerning the transfer of personnel from one company to another. Pursuant to Labour Law, as amended, the transfer of personnel that does not involve the transfer of the company's establishment requires the express written consent of each employee who is being transferred.

[227] Even when the employees accept the transfer, both the buyer and seller will remain jointly and severally liable for all obligations resulting from the employees' prior labour relationships with the seller

[228] The statute of limitations for such past obligations is ten years for social security contributions and two years for labour obligations in general.

Acquisitions: Remedies after Completion

Specific Legislation

[229] Argentine law does not provide specific remedies in the case of a contract for the acquisition of an enterprise, whether it is structured as a share or an asset deal. The statutory remedies available to the purchaser of an enterprise are, in general, those applicable to any purchase of goods. Although a specific statute regulates the procedure for the acquisition of a going concern in which all the essential assets of a business are purchased, the statute is principally aimed at protecting the seller's creditors and does not grant any additional remedies to the buyer.

Asset Deal

[230] Argentine law grants to the buyer a guarantee against eviction (or 'warranty of title') and a guarantee against latent defects, as statutory remedies applicable even in the absence of specific provisions in the purchase contract. Eviction occurs if the buyer is deprived by operation of law, in whole or in part, of its right to the goods purchased, or is disturbed in the ownership, possession or use of the goods purchased. Under Argentine law, the guarantee against eviction protects the buyer against dispossession by operation of law of any kind of goods and not merely land or rental property, and also against third-party claims on IT rights, except when the seller has adjusted to the specifics granted to buyer (pursuant to Article 1,044 of the Civil and Commercial Code).

[231] Latent defects are hidden or concealed defects that existed at the time of purchase and that render the goods unsuitable for the use intended, due to either structural or functional reasons, so that the buyer would not have bought the goods or would have paid a lower price for them, had the buyer been aware of their existence.

[232] In general, the remedies available to the buyer consist of:

(a) in the case of eviction, the reimbursement of the price paid (even if the goods purchased decreased in value or deteriorated due to force majeure or the buyer's negligence), without interest, and the payment of damages; and
(b) In the case of latent defects, at the option of the buyer:
   (i) The reimbursement of the price in exchange for the return of the defective goods to the seller.
   (ii) The partial refund of the price to reflect the reduction in the value of the goods due to the defect.

[233] In the case of latent defects, the seller is not liable for damages unless: (i) the seller knew of or should have known of the existence of such defect, that is to say, that the seller should act with sufficient diligence by means of, for example, negotiating the purchase price with having such defects in mind; and (ii) if the transfer of the goods has been made at the buyer's own risk.

[234] In principle, both remedies apply only to the individual product that is subject to the eviction or has the latent defect. However, when the transaction involves the purchase of two or more products and the product that is affected by the eviction or the latent defect is of such importance that the buyer would not have purchased the other product without it, the buyer has the option to seek redress for the affected product only or for all the products purchased in the transaction.

Share Purchase Transaction

[235] According to a majority of the doctrine and court decisions, defects in the assets of the target company would not be considered defects in the shares, even if the buyer purchased all of the outstanding shares of the company.

[236] Argentine courts have maintained that 'the seller of a shareholding only transfers its rights as a shareholder and does not respond to the existence of hidden debts or other irregularities (with respect to the company's net worth) except where such liability has been expressly agreed upon'. In particular, one court has pointed out that shares are only securities representing the capital of a corporation and that it makes no sense to refer to 'latent defects' in this respect.

[237] Another court has expressly applied this principle to the acquisition of a large percentage of the capital of a company, holding that the buyer must take the necessary measures to avoid hidden contingencies. This court went so far as to hold that individuals or legal entities that frequently enter into commercial transactions must either adhere to the due diligence standard of a business person or assume the risk of suffering damages as a result of their failure to perform such due diligence.

[238] Nevertheless, as one author has pointed out, the conclusion that the seller is not liable with respect to the value given the company's assets raises fairness concerns (*razones de equidad*). In this vein, it is argued that if a remedy exists only to the extent an express contractual provision has been violated, a benefit will inure to the party who has acted contrary to the overriding principles of good faith and fair dealing set forth in Article 961 of the Civil and Commercial Code, where both provisions of which may be considered by a court when adjudicating the availability of a remedy. Article 961 of the Civil and Commercial Code provides that: 'Contracts should be entered into, interpreted and performed in good faith. [The parties] are bound not only by what is formally expressed, but also for all of the consequences that may be considered covered by them, with the scope under which a reasonable and careful contractor would have contracted.'

Cancellation of the Transaction

[239] Articles 1,087 and 1,088 of the Civil and Commercial Code grant the rights to request termination (*derecho de resolución*) of any contract that involves reciprocal obligations in the event of a breach of a material obligation by one of the parties. Also, Article 1,086 provides the right for the parties of a transaction to expressly agree on the resolution of the contract in the event of generic or specific breaches duly identified. In order to terminate the contract, the non-breaching party must notify the other party that the contract will terminate unless the breach is cured within fifteen days, except that due to standard practice or the nature of the transaction, a shorter term results applicable. Alternatively, the non-breaching party may petition a court to have the contract terminated, in which case the other party will be precluded from performing in order to avoid termination. If the breach is not remedied within such period, the contract is deemed terminated by operation of law.

[240] Termination of the contract in this manner will have retroactive effects between the parties so that, in the case of a sale, the seller will be entitled to the return of the goods sold and damages or, if the goods have not yet been delivered to the buyer, to retain them. The right to the return of the goods cannot be enforced if, after the initial purchase, the goods have been acquired by a third-party in good faith and for consideration.

[241] In the absence of an express termination provision in the contract, the breach of a confidentiality, non-compete or any other clause that is deemed non-essential would not give rise to a right of termination but only to a claim for damages.

[242] The guarantee against eviction applies to an acquisition of shares as well. Therefore, a seller implicitly guarantees title to the shares sold and should be held liable if there is a defect in the title. Eviction would entitle the buyer to the reimbursement of the price and damages.

[243] The right of the buyer to seek termination in the case of latent defects in the assets of the target business would depend on whether the acquisition has been structured as an asset or a share deal.

[244] In an asset deal, the existence of a latent defect in a single asset would only entitle the buyer, at their discretion, to obtain a refund of the price of the defective asset or a partial refund to reflect the decrease in value of the defective asset. The former option would extend to all the assets purchased only if the importance of the defective asset is so great that the buyer would not have purchased the other assets without it. If the acquisition were a share deal, defects in the assets of the target company would not be deemed defects of the shares.

[245] Defects must be substantial to allow the buyer to terminate a transaction. The buyer may waive the implicit right of termination granted by Articles 1,087 and 1,088 of the Civil and Commercial Code that is discussed above. The buyer may also waive the right to seek remedy in the case of eviction or latent defects, but in no event shall such waiver limit the buyer's right to seek redress if the act that gave rise to the eviction or the existence of the latent defect was caused or known by the seller. The buyer is not entitled to a remedy if the seller informed the buyer of the existence of the latent defect prior to the execution of the acquisition agreement.

[246] Article 1,089 of the Civil and Commercial Code states that termination takes place by operation of law once the fifteen-day period (or a shorter one, if appropriate) has elapsed without performance by the breaching party. Once termination occurs, the contract may not be reinstated unilaterally by the party that sought the termination. Likewise, the party that elects to request termination through the courts is prevented afterwards from substituting such petition for one requesting compliance.

[247] Argentine law contemplates other grounds for termination, including fundamental error, fraud, violence, threats and state of need provided some circumstances are given in each case.

Damages

[248] The seller is not liable for damages in connection with the existence of latent defects in the assets sold, unless (i) the seller knew of or should have known of the existence of such defect, that is to say, that the seller should act with sufficient diligence by means of, for example, negotiating the purchase price with having such defects in mind; and (ii) if the transfer of the goods has been made at the buyer's own risk.

[249] The scope and extent of damages caused by latent defects in the assets sold are governed by the general rules on damages of the Civil Code. Those rules classify damages as direct (*inmediatos*) or consequential (*mediatos*). Direct damages are those that normally result from the non-compliance in the natural and ordinary course. Consequential damages are those that occur because of the combination of the non-compliance with another event or act. The seller will only be liable for consequential damages if the seller acted wilfully. However, the liability of the seller will not extend to consequential damages that are unpredictable.

[250] In the absence of an express guarantee, the buyer of shares is not entitled to collect damages for latent defects in the assets of the target company. In the case that the buyer loses the title to the shares by eviction, damages will be payable by the seller to the purchaser.

[251] In the case of latent defects in the assets, the buyer may not claim damages if it seeks a reduction in price, but only when it elects to return the assets sold against a full refund. Instead of seeking termination for non-compliance with an essential obligation, the buyer has the option to request compliance plus damages.

Contractual Clauses on Remedies

[252] As explained, Argentine courts have held that latent defects in the assets are not deemed defects in the shares. Therefore, it is advisable to include a provision in the contract to that effect if such protection is important to the buyer. The seller should guarantee the characteristics and or the quality of the assets underlying the shares sold. This guarantee is implicitly made when the seller represents in the purchase agreement that the goods sold lack defects or that the goods have certain qualities. While the lack of a guaranteed quality or defect is not a hidden defect in the strict sense, such circumstance would entitle the buyer to the same remedies.

[253] The acquisition of a company is a highly complex transaction; therefore termination after the closing should be contemplated only for the most pressing reasons. As a practical matter, and considering that in the time elapsed since the takeover the buyer is likely to have changed the structure, personnel and method of operations of the company, it would be difficult to agree on a termination right and proceeding acceptable to both parties. As a matter of practice, a buyer, for whom compensation in the form of a price reduction would not be sufficient, would be well advised to emphasize protective measures through a thorough due diligence investigation.

[254] Termination should not limit appropriate claims for damages. In principle, any damage payments should be payable to the buyer and not to the target company.

Guarantees on Receivables of the Target Company by the Seller

[255] In practice, it is not common to find in Argentine transactions a carve-out of indemnification on accounts receivable in the case of unexpected insolvency of the debtors. This would depend on the bargaining power of the parties.

[256] In general, the purchaser will be responsible for the collection of accounts receivable and should be in a position to prove its 'best efforts' in connection with such an undertaking. Some form of participation of the seller in the proceedings is likely. Sellers agreeing to some form of settlement arrangement is advisable. The seller's guarantee will lapse upon any settlement reached without the seller's consent.

Escrow Accounts

[257] Depending on the nature of the expected claims, it may be efficient to set up an escrow account managed by a trustee to disburse payments to cover such claims or relied on such purpose for the awards of the arbitration. Frequently, disbursements by the trustee are made in a manner similar to disbursements under a letter of credit (i.e., not on demand by the buyer but against presentation of certain evidence such as a statement signed by independent auditors). To the extent that the existence and the amount of such claims were easily determinable, the use of an escrow account could prove advantageous.

[258] Normally, this will depend on the currency in which the transaction is made and is a matter of negotiation. Since inflation in Argentina was high for many years, most M&A transactions are generally agreed using US dollars as a benchmark for all the financial aspects.

Statute of Limitations

[259] The statute of limitations is: (i) three years for claims for damages due to breach of contract and seeking compliance with contract obligations; and (ii) one year for claims in connection with the existence of latent defects in the assets purchased. The Civil and Commercial Code expressly states that all provisions related to the statute of limitations cannot be amended by agreement of the parties (pursuant to Article 2,533).

[260] The statute of limitations for federal tax liabilities is five years counted as from 1 January of the following year in which the tax return should be filed.

[261] The deadline of the statute of limitation may be met by submitting a claim to the court or the arbitration tribunal, or by the express or implied admission of the debtor.

ANTITRUST/COMPETITION ISSUES

Relevant Legislation and Competent Authorities

[262] In 1994, when the Argentine Constitution was amended, protection for competition against any kind of market distortion, and control of natural and legal monopolies were included as a constitutional right.

[263] On 9 May 2018 the Argentine Congress sanctioned Law No. 27,442 (the 'Antitrust Law'), set to replace the former antitrust law, Law No. 25,156, as amended by Law No. 26,993. On 24 May 2018 the new Antitrust Law entered into effect and, on the same day, Regulatory Decree No. 480/2018 was published in the Official Gazette, by means of which the executive branch regulated certain core points of the Antitrust Law.

[264] In accordance to the former antitrust laws, the merger control system established by the Antitrust Law sets out that certain transactions must be notified for clearance in the event that there is a change of control, economic thresholds are met and no exemptions apply.

[265] The Antitrust Law creates a new enforcement authority: the National Competition Authority (hereinafter the 'NCA'), a new decentralized and self-regulated entity within the scope of the executive branch.

[266] The NCA has not yet been created. In the meantime, the current two-tier regulatory system continues to apply as with the previous regime, which is composed of the Antitrust Commission, which was designed to do technical reviews on mergers and investigations and to issue recommendations to the Secretary of Trade, which would be the ultimate ruling body.

[267] The NCA will be composed by the Antitrust Tribunal, the Secretariat of Instruction of Anticompetitive Behaviours and the Secretariat of Economic Concentrations.

[268] The Antitrust Tribunal will be composed of five members, a minimum of two of whom must be lawyers and a minimum of two of whom must be economists. The NCA's members will be appointed by the Executive Power after a pre-selection process carried out by the Legislative Power. This Antitrust Tribunal will be in charge of imposing sanctions contained in the new Antitrust Law, issuing resolutions on preliminary defences, deciding on the approval of mergers and carrying out any market investigations that are deemed pertinent. In addition, the tribunal will impose fees that individuals and/or companies will have to pay when submitting merger notifications. This is the decision-making role currently held by the Secretary of Trade.

[269] The main purpose of the Secretariat of Instruction of Anticompetitive Behaviours will be to receive and process investigations of anticompetitive conduct in order to give the Antitrust Tribunal recommendations regarding necessary sanctions. The Antitrust Law empowered the Secretariat of Instruction of Anticompetitive Behaviours to perform dawn raids with a judicial notice, among many other powers.

[270] For its part, the Secretariat of Economic Concentrations has, as its main objective, receiving and processing advisory opinion and merger dockets that are filed with the NCA. Furthermore, it has the authority to decide on the approval of those mergers that qualify for a fast-track review process, the requirements of which are to be determined by the Executive Power. In addition, the Secretariat of Economic Concentration is vested with, *inter alia*, the following powers: to approve or reject transactions of economic concentration for which notice is received; to study and analyse market conditions; to receive, analyse and decide the advisory opinions under Article 10 of the Antitrust Law.

[271] As regards the applicable procedural law, supplementary to the Antitrust Law, it should be noted that, before the Antitrust Law was enacted, the former antitrust law set out that in those cases not foreseen by the law, the provisions of the Administrative Procedural Law (Law No. 19,549) were to be applied. This rule changed with the enactment of the Antitrust Law. Under the current system, pursuant to Article 79 of the Antitrust Law, it is the Criminal Code and the Criminal Procedural Code which applies to those cases not set out in the Antitrust Law.

Scope of the Controls

[272] Article 1 of Antitrust Law prohibits certain acts or conducts relating to the production and exchange of goods and services if they limit, restrict, falsify or distort competition, or if they constitute an abuse of a dominant position in a market, provided that in both cases, such acts or conducts may cause harm to the general economic interest. Although such behaviour or conduct is not unlawful per se, it is not necessary to cause actual damage: it is unlawful if the conduct is likely to cause harm to the general economic interest.

[273] Antitrust Law is applicable to all individuals and entities that carry out business activities within Argentina and to those who carry out business activities abroad, to the extent that their acts, activities or agreements may have any effects in the Argentine market.

[274] Foreign-to-foreign transactions may involve direct or indirect transfers of control in Argentina and may, therefore, require advance notice to the NCA. Since Antitrust Law has accepted the widely recognized 'effects theory', foreign-to-foreign transactions having an impact on the Argentine market are subject to its provisions. The NCA has authority to analyse the local effects of any foreign-to-foreign transaction since the Antitrust Law is applicable to all individuals and entities that carry on business activities within Argentina and to those who carry on business activities abroad, to the extent that their acts, activities or agreements may have any effects on the Argentine market.

Change of Control

[275] Antitrust Law provides that certain mergers and acquisitions and bulk asset sales resulting in economic concentrations (*concentraciones económicas*) require, under certain circumstances, the prior approval of the NCA.

[276] Certain transactions are deemed as economic concentrations when they result in the assumption of control of one or more companies by means of any of the following acts:

(i) Mergers.
(ii) Transfers of businesses.
(iii) Acquisitions of shares or equity interests, any interest thereto, convertible debt securities or securities that grant to the acquirer the control of, or a substantial influence over, the issuer.
(iv) Any other agreement or act through which assets of a company are transferred to a person or economic group or which gives decision-making control over the ordinary or extraordinary decisions of management of a company.

[277] To determine whether a (be it a local one or a foreign-to-foreign) transaction requires advance notice to the NCA, Antitrust Law provides for two thresholds, and an interpretation of the NCA provides a third threshold. The third threshold is applicable only if the companies concerned imports into Argentina.

[278] The three thresholds are determined under three different tests. If the result of the first is higher than 100 000 000 Adjustable Units (equivalent to ARS2 000 000 000), the second and the third thresholds must also be applied. If the first threshold is not met, the rest of the thresholds are not applicable and the transaction is not subject to the antitrust filing requirements.

Volume of Business

[279] Antitrust Law states that only those transactions which entail a change of control over an undertaking where the aggregate volume of business of the companies involved exceeds 100 000 000 Adjustable Units (equivalent to ARS2 000 000 000) in Argentina require advance notice and approval by the NCA. Please note that currently 1 Adjustable Unit is ARS20. Adjustable Units will be adjusted on an annual basis.

[280] The volume of business is equal to the gross sale of products or services during the preceding fiscal year arising from their ordinary businesses net of discount sales, Value Added Tax (VAT) and other direct taxes. The volume of business arises only from the economic activities performed in Argentina and the worldwide turnover that the economic group may have is not taken into account for those purposes.

[281] To calculate the volume of business, the total volume of business of the target company (the company being acquired), the buyer and all those companies under the control of the buyer must be included, as well as of any companies which directly or indirectly control the buyer.

[282] If the total amount of the volume of business for the preceding fiscal year in Argentina is 100 000 000 Adjustable Units or more, the principal threshold provided in the Antitrust Law is met. Advance notice of the transaction must be filed with to the NCA and the other two tests referred to below will have to be applied.

[283] On the contrary, if the total amount of the volume of business is lower than 100 000 000 Adjustable Units, the transaction does not require filing with the NCA and the other two thresholds do not need to be applied since the principal threshold provided in the Antitrust Law has not been met. In this case a review of the transaction is not required under the Antitrust Law.

Size of the Transaction

[284] The size of the transaction's threshold is derived from one of the exemptions referred to in the Antitrust Law. The Antitrust Law provides that even when the volume of business of the transaction is higher than 100 000 000 Adjustable Units, where the value of the transaction in Argentina and the value of the assets in Argentina are each lower than 20 000 000 Adjustable Units (equivalent to ARS400 000 000), the transaction is exempted from the previous antitrust filing. To be eligible for this exemption, the parties involved must not have participated in similar transactions involving an aggregate amount of 20 000 000 Adjustable Units during the preceding twelve months or 60 000 000 Adjustable Units (equivalent to ARS1 200 000 000) during the preceding thirty-six months.

[285] In the case of foreign-to-foreign transactions, the information that must be evaluated for the purpose of this test is:

(i) The total value of the foreign-to-foreign element of the transaction in Argentina, in cases where the foreign-to-foreign transaction includes the acquisition of stock/quotas or any other interest or participation in Argentina.

(ii) Involved in Argentina in cases where the foreign-to-foreign transaction includes the acquisition of certain assets in Argentina.

Size of the Effects

[286] The size of the effect is used to measure the effects that a foreign-to-foreign transaction may have in Argentina. This test may be applied only if the parties involved in the foreign-to-foreign transaction have sales/imports into Argentina.

[287] The Antitrust Commission has issued an interpretation that the effects in the local market of a foreign-to-foreign transaction must be substantial, normal and regular for advance antitrust clearance to be required.

[288] There is no precise rule to determine when the effects can be considered substantial, normal and regular. The Antitrust Commission has decided several cases based on: (a) the market shares of the products imported by the parties involved in the foreign-to-foreign transaction; and (b) the regularity of the imports over a certain period of time (the last preceding three years). The effects are substantial if the exports into Argentina represent a significant percentage of the total relevant market for that specific product (but the specific percentage is not clear). The effects are regular and normal if the imports have been constant during the last preceding three years.

Exemptions Provided in the Antitrust Law

[289] When the three thresholds mentioned above have been met, the Antitrust Law provides for certain specific exemptions to the antitrust pre-filing obligation. The exemptions are as follows:

(i) Acquisitions of companies, when the purchaser already holds more than 50% of the shares, provided that it does not entail a change in the nature of control.

(ii) Acquisitions of bonds, debentures, non-voting shares or debt securities of companies.

(iii) Acquisitions of only one company by only one foreign company that does not have any assets or shares of other companies in Argentina (known as the 'first landing' exemption). In case the foreign company is active in the country by means of exports, the 'first landing' exception could still be invoked if such exports were not substantial, regular and predictable during the last 36 months, but a case-by-case analysis should be carried out.

(iv) Acquisitions of wound up and liquidated companies (which have not performed any activity in Argentina during the preceding calendar year).

(v) Gratuitous transfers of goods to the Argentine State, the Provinces, Municipalities and the City of Buenos Aires.

(vi) Transfer of goods to and among mandatory heirs, by acts carried out between living persons or as a result of death.

Process: Mechanics

[290] Notices must be submitted on the so-called Forms F-1 and F-2. Depending on the size of the local transaction, the parties may be advised to file simultaneously Forms F-1 and F-2. Should the NCA deem that the information filed is insufficient to analyse the competition effects of the foreign-to-foreign transaction, it may request additional information through a 'tailor-made' Form F-3.

[291] According to Article 9 of Regulatory Decree No. 480/2018, antitrust filing is optional for the seller. Consequently, the responsibility for filing now falls only on the acquirer. However, the very same article states that the antitrust authority may request the seller's participation during the proceedings.

[292] The prescribed forms require a substantial amount of information to be provided. Given the scope and complexity of the forms and of the short time for filing, parties may be well advised to focus on the notification requirements at an early stage in the planning and implementation process for a merger or an acquisition.

[293] While some of the information to be provided is relatively simple to obtain (agreements, financial statements, etc.), other information may be difficult to obtain and time-consuming. This is particularly true for the detailed information parties must provide to identify the products involved and the relevant market.

[294] Information for which confidential treatment is requested should be labelled 'Confidential'.

[295] If a party considers that the NCA will not need certain information to assess the transaction, it can ask to waive the requirement to provide it. Parties may also wish to approach the NCA at an early stage on a confidential and informal basis to seek agreement to reduce the amount of information to be provided in the form. Also, in the event of serious doubts on whether the economic transaction requires notice, the parties may approach the NCA and request an advisory opinion on the specific case.

[296] Pursuant to Article 33 of the Antitrust Law, the notifying parties have to pay a filing fee, which will range between 5 000 and 20 000 Adjustable Units (equivalent to ARS100 000 and 400 000). However, no fees are at present being imposed.

[297] Article 9 of the Antitrust Law set up a suspensive regime in which the parties would not be able to close the transaction prior to its approval. This is the most relevant departure that the new Antitrust Law made from the previous system, in which parties could close the transaction and file for notification up to one week afterwards. The Antitrust Law, in Article 55(d), has established fines for gun-jumping, fines which had hitherto never existed in Argentine merger control proceedings. However, it must be noted that the suspensive regime will only become effective as of one year after the creation of the NCA.

[298] Until the suspensive effect becomes effective, notice of the economic concentrations within the definition described above must be submitted for clearance prior to or within one week after the earlier of: (i) the date that any transfer effectively occurs; or (ii) the publication of any cash tender or exchange offer.

[299] Pursuant to Article 55(d), late filing and gun-jumping will be subject to daily fines of up to 0.1% of the consolidated annual turnover in Argentina of the notifying companies or, if such criterion could not be used, daily fines of currently up to 750 000 Adjustable Units (equivalent to ARS15 000 000).

[300] Article 9 of the Antitrust Law sets out that any transaction subject to merger control before the NCA will not generate effects vis-à-vis the parties or third parties until it has been approved by said body, either expressly or tacitly. However, that very same Article of the Antitrust Law also sets out that the notification must be carried out before or up to one week after the effective closing of the transaction.

[301] Once the notice has been submitted, the enforcement authority must decide within forty-five business days whether to: (i) unconditionally approve the transaction; (ii) approve the transaction but impose conditions; or (iii) reject the transaction. If no decision is issued by the enforcement authority within forty-five business days from the filing of the application and relevant documents, the transaction shall be considered tacitly approved.

[302] In the cases of economic concentrations between companies that perform activities in regulated markets, the enforcement authority will extend the period for thirty days more in order to obtain the opinion on the economic concentration from the relevant regulatory agency.

[303] Notwithstanding the above, please note that the enforcement authority is currently enforcing a 'stop-the-clock' interpretation that entails that the first request of information by the regulator in a merger control proceeding suspends these terms. As a result, the enforcement authority is currently demanding between six to nine months in order to analyse transactions. In addition, a summary proceeding is foreseen for certain concentrations (fast-track), to be regulated in the future.

Type of Analysis: Submission of Remedies

[304] The guidelines referring to the Control of the Economic Concentrations provided by Resolution No. 208/18 of the Secretary of Trade (hereinafter the 'Guidelines') establish that horizontal mergers would not trigger any preliminary concern in competition if the market share of the combined entity is below 20% of the market. In addition, vertical mergers would not entail any competitive concern if the market shares are below 30% both in the upstream and downstream markets. However, a case-by-case analysis should be carried out.

[305] In the event that the enforcement authority deems that the transaction submitted to review may generate a concern, it can request certain remedies from the notifying parties. These remedies can either be structural (such as a divestment) or behavioural (such as price monitoring or access to competitors). Remedies are usually negotiated with the notifying parties. As of late, the regulator has shown a special emphasis on price control remedies, in order for the parties not to increase prices.

Request for an Advisory Opinion

[306] Article 10 of the Antitrust Law state that parties to a transaction are entitled to file a voluntary petition for an advisory opinion before the competent authority.

[307] Resolution No. 26/2006 of the Secretary of Technical Coordination of the Ministry of Economy and Production (currently the Secretary of Trade) rules the proceedings to request an advisory opinion. In order to request the advisory opinion, the parties have to describe the transaction and explain why, under their interpretation, the transaction is exempted from the prior antitrust control.

[308] The enforcement authority must analyse the information filed by the parties and may request additional information, if necessary. The parties are given five days to respond to the request for additional information. If the parties do not respond to the request for additional information, the petition will be considered as not filed, unless the parties provide a reason for failing to respond. If no additional information is requested or if the parties comply with the requirements, the tribunal must issue its opinion within the term of ten business days from the day in which the parties filed the petition.

[309] Additionally, the Regulatory Decree 480/2018 establishes that the advisory opinion issued by the enforcement authority will have a duration of six months, renewable only once at the request of the involved companies for justified reasons. In case the transaction brought to consultation is not carried out within the said term, a new request must be filed in the terms of Article 10 of the Antitrust Law.

[310] It should be noted that the enforcement authority is currently demanding between six months and a year to issue resolutions in advisory opinions.

[311] As per section 10 of the Antitrust Law, the advisory opinion issued by the NCA is indisputable.

[312] The legal deadlines will be suspended upon filing of the petition and until the advisory opinion becomes final.

Penalties and Sanctions

[313] The NCA may apply fines and request a judicial order to liquidate or require the spin-off of companies infringing the provisions of the Antitrust Law. The directors, managers, administrators, internal auditors and members of the supervisory committee, attorneys-in-fact and legal representatives of such entities may be held jointly and severally liable with the infringing entity.

[314] In the event that the enforcement authority decides to investigate on the reasons for which a transaction has not been notified, it will open a Preliminary Diligence, by means of which it will request information on the grounds for which the transaction was not notified. Please note that should the enforcement authority consider that the transaction should have been notified, it will impose a late filing fee as well as issue the order for the filing of the transaction.

Anticompetitive Restraints

Ancillary Restraints under Argentine Case Law

[315] These types of provisions are valid as long as they comply with certain rules issued by the NCA when analysing merger control cases. The tribunal bases its case law on the rules set out by the European Commission's case law on non-compete obligations. As a general rule, in the case of sales in which goodwill is transferred, a non-compete obligation of two years has been accepted by the enforcement authority. In those cases in which a transfer of know-how is also included in the transfer, a longer term of five years has been accepted by the NCA. Both of the above-mentioned terms shall be valid as of the effective transfer of the shares and/or the assets and/or business.

[316] In both of these cases there must be a correlation between the assets and/or business being transferred with the non-compete obligation. Those restrictions to competition, that go beyond the scope of the business that is being transferred, have been considered as non-enforceable by the enforcement authority and in merger control proceedings must be amended in order for that transaction to be approved.

[317] Furthermore, there must also be a correlation between the business being transferred and the geographical scope of the non-compete obligation. Thus, the non-compete obligation cannot be set out with a greater scope than that of the undertaking over which control is being acquired.

[318] In the case of Joint Ventures, the non-compete obligation can be set out for the entire duration of the Joint Venture and the enforcement authority has already accepted these types of provisions. Furthermore, the non-compete obligation must also be referred only to the products and/or services offered by the Joint Venture itself and not those of the parent companies, since that could be construed as a market allocation. An additional term for a short period of time (i.e., six months) has been accepted post-Joint Venture. As to the geographic scope, this must be restricted to the geographical areas in which the Joint Venture will operate.

Description of Prohibited Practices

[319] Under the previous antitrust regime (i.e., Law No. 25,156) there were no anticompetitive behaviours per se since the current or potential damage to the general economic interest had to be determined in order to consider a conduct as anticompetitive. The new Antitrust Law presumes that there are certain behaviours which are absolute restrictions to competition ('hardcore' cartels), in order to enhance cartel prosecution. These agreements shall be deemed null and will not generate any effects.

[320] Those behaviours are now listed under section 2 of the Antitrust Law, namely:

(a) to fix, directly or indirectly, the price of the purchase or sale of products and/ or services;
(b) to establish obligations of (a) manufacturing, distributing, buying or commercializing a limited amount of goods and/or (b) to provide a limited number, volume or frequency of services;
(c) to divide, distribute or horizontally impose areas, portions or segments of the markets, clients or supply sources; or
(d) to establish or coordinate submissions or abstentions in public tenders.

Additionally, the Antitrust Law also prosecutes certain conducts that may entail an abuse of a dominant position. In such cases, the perpetrator must have: (a) a dominant position in the relevant market; (b) the conduct must distort competition in that market either by exploitative or exclusionary means; and (c) there must be harm to the general economic interest.

Leniency Program

[321] The Antitrust Law incorporates a leniency program in order to facilitate the investigation of 'hardcore' cartels by establishing two possible run-to-the-door scenarios for those who adhere to the benefit: full exemption or reduction of fines, as well as immunity from certain criminal sanctions and damages, with certain specific exceptions.

[322] In order for the full exemption to apply, the petitioner must (i) be the first among those involved in the conduct to apply and supply evidence, (ii) immediately cease the anticompetitive action (iii), cooperate with the NCA during the proceedings, (iv) not destroy evidence of anticompetitive behaviour, and (v) not disclose the intention to adhere to the benefit. If the petitioner is not the first to adhere to the benefit, they may be eligible for a reduction of between 50% and 20% of the fine if they provide additional evidence to the investigation. The filing can be made at any time until a formal accusation is served on the parties.

[323] Article 60 section (d) of the new Antitrust Law also introduced a supplementary benefit ('leniency plus') for the petitioner who, not being able to adhere to the benefit during the substantiation of the investigation, reveals and recognizes a second cartel in a market. In addition to the exemption granted for such conduct, the benefit will also consist of a reduction of one-third of the sanction or fine that would have otherwise been imposed because of participation in the first conduct.

Dominant Position

[324] For the purposes of the Antitrust Law, 'dominant position' includes situations where one or more persons are the only offeror or demanding party of a specific product within the Argentine market or in one or more regions of the world. Even if that person is not the only offeror or demanding party in any of those markets, they can still be deemed to be holding a dominant position if they are not subject to substantial competition or if, by means of a vertical or horizontal integration, they are in a position to harm the economic viability of a competitor in the market.

Penalties and Sanctions

[325] The NCA may apply fines and request a judicial order to liquidate or require the spin-off of companies infringing the provisions of the Antitrust Law. The directors, managers, administrators, internal auditors and members of the supervisory committee, attorneys-in-fact and legal representatives of such entities may be held jointly and severally liable with the infringing entity.

[326] As regards anticompetitive behaviours, the Antitrust Law establishes that the infringing parties can be fined by the higher of the following two methods:

- fines up to 30% of the volume of business of the last fiscal year, associated to the products and/or services involved in the perpetuation of the anticompetitive conduct, multiplied by the years of duration of the conduct, which, in turn, should not exceed 30% of the consolidated volume of business generated in Argentina in the last fiscal year of the group to which the perpetrator belongs; or
- up to double the economic benefit reported by the anticompetitive conduct. If the calculation of the fine is not viable under any of the methods described above, the fine could be of up to 200 000 000 Adjustable Units, equivalent to ARS4 000 000 000.

[327] In addition, Article 55 sub-section e) of the Antitrust Law establishes the possibility of being suspended in the National Registry of Suppliers of the State for a maximum of five years. For those involved in bid-rigging activities, the suspension might be up to eight years.

Appeals

[328] The new Antitrust Law eliminates the previous *solve et repete* system, which entailed that fines had to be paid in order to have access to a judicial appeal. As such, these will now only have to be paid upon confirmation by the courts. However, the party appealing must pay guarantee insurance on the imposed fine to appeal (pursuant to Article 67).

[329] The discussion regarding the applicable Court of Appeals followed a similar path of irresolution in the past. Over the last decade, the question as to whether the Federal Court of Appeals on Civil and Commercial Matters or the Argentine Court of Appeals on Criminal Economic Matters was the appropriate appellate court generated a lot of discussions, and both appellate bodies had issued resolutions on matters arising from the Antitrust Law. The Amendment Law of 2014 was supposed to resolve this; it created an Argentine Court of Appeals on Consumer Relations to deal with consumer-related matters, including antitrust cases. However, said Court of Appeals was ultimately never created and the divergence remained.

[330] The Antitrust Law has addressed this issue by establishing that the Federal Court of Appeals on Civil and Commercial Matters is the applicable Court of Appeals and creating a specialized chamber for antitrust matters within the said court.

TAXATION ASPECTS

Purchase of Shares

Income Tax

[331] Capital gains derived by an Argentine company from the sale of shares are subject to Argentine income tax as prescribed by the applicable regulations, and the payment of such tax is normally borne by the seller.

[332] The tax is calculated on the net income of the taxpayer at the end of the fiscal year involved. In order to calculate the net taxable income, the taxpayer is entitled to deduct all necessary expenses incurred in obtaining that taxable income.

Capital gains derived by Argentine individuals from the sale of shares are subject to Argentine income tax at a flat rate of 15%.

Pursuant to a recent amendment to the Income Tax Law, only the income arising from the sale, transfer or disposition of shares, securities representing shares and certificates of deposit of shares that are carried out through stock exchanges or stock markets authorized by the Argentine Securities and Exchange Commission (the 'CNV' after its acronym in Spanish) will be exempt.

This exemption will also be applicable to foreign beneficiaries to the extent that said beneficiaries do not reside in and the funds do not come from non-cooperative jurisdictions. The exemption will also be applicable to public securities issued by the national, provincial, municipal or the City of Buenos Aires governments, negotiable obligations and representative shares or deposit certificates shares and other securities provided that such securities have been issued by entities domiciled or located in Argentina

[333] If the seller of the shares is a foreign resident, the profits from the sale, exchange or disposal of shares, securities, bonds, are taxed by Argentine income tax.

[334] In such cases, the Argentine Income Tax Law presumes a net profit of 90% on the amount of the transaction. Since the tax rate is 15%, the effective rate is 13.5%. The entity may choose to pay 15% on the difference between the gross profit of the transaction less the costs incurred in the country in order to obtain and maintain it and the deductions allowed by the Income Tax Law.

[335] When shares, securities or bonds that belong to a foreign individual or entity are sold to or exchanged with a foreign individual or entity, the law provides that the seller is obliged to collect and pay the tax.

Indirect Transfer of Shares: The ITL establishes the presumption of income from Argentina when non-Argentine residents transfer shares and participations of foreign entities whose underlying assets are fully or partly Argentine. This new concept is in the unnumbered article following Article 13 of Income Tax Law and is entitled 'indirect disposal of assets located in t national territory'.

This concept establishes that when a non-Argentine resident transfers shares, quotas, participations and other rights representative of the capital or equity of an entity incorporated, domiciled or located abroad, the resulting income will be considered as Argentine source income as long as the following conditions prevail:

(1) The value of the shares, participations or rights of the foreign entity, at the time of sale or in any of the twelve (12) previous months, represent at least 30% of the value of the assets that the entity owns directly or indirectly in the Argentine Republic.
   Argentine assets will be valued at current average cost and will include:
   (i) the shares, rights, quotas or other participation certificates in the ownership, control or profits of a company, fund, trust or other entity incorporated in the Argentine Republic;
   (ii) permanent establishments in the Argentine Republic belonging to a non-resident person or entity;
   (iii) other assets of any nature located in the Argentine Republic or rights over them.

(2) Sold shares, participations or rights of the foreign entity represent 10% of the equity of that entity, at the time of their disposal or in any of the twelve previous months.
   For this purpose, disposals are included both by the individual itself and those made jointly with entities over which it has control or a relationship, with spouse, cohabitant or with other taxpayers linked by family relationship, ascending, descending or collateral line, by kinship or affinity, up to third degree inclusive.

Other Taxes

[336] The transfer of shares of an Argentine corporation is neither subject to VAT nor to turnover tax.

[337] Provided certain requirements are met, the transfer of shares of a company can be carried out without triggering off any tax liability in Argentina, except stamp tax, when applicable.

Taxes Applicable on the Holding of Shares

[338] Personal Assets Tax Law No. 23,966, as amended, creates a personal assets tax on individuals domiciled in Argentina and abroad. Individuals domiciled in Argentina are liable for personal assets tax upon their worldwide assets, while individuals not domiciled in Argentina are only liable for this tax upon their assets located in Argentina. Company shares, among other securities, are deemed to be located in Argentina when issued by a legal entity domiciled in Argentina.

[339] Although the personal assets tax is only imposed on individuals, there is an irrefutable presumption that shares owned by any kind of foreign entity are owned by an individual domiciled abroad and are, therefore, subject to the tax. The Argentine issuer company is liable for the payment of such tax at a 0.25% the value of the shares

It is entitled to seek recovery from the foreign entity. Certain conventions for the avoidance of double taxation entered into between Argentine and other countries could prevent the applicability of this tax.

Transfer of Assets

Income Tax

[340] Income tax applies at a rate of 30% (for the fiscal years 2018 and 2019 and 25% for the next years) on the difference between the price and the cost estimated pursuant to Argentine tax regulations. In certain cases, the cost of the assets may be adjusted for inflation.

[341] Income tax is normally borne by the seller. The tax is calculated on the net income of the taxpayer at the end of the fiscal year involved. In order to calculate the net taxable income the taxpayer is entitled to deduct all necessary expenses incurred in obtaining that taxable income. Losses incurred during any fiscal year may be carried forward and set off against taxable income obtained during the following five fiscal years.

VALUE ADDED TAX

[342] VAT applies at a general rate of 21%, with some exceptions for real estate. Besides, sales and imports of capital goods are subject to VAT at a lower tax rate of 10.5%.

[343] VAT is payable by the purchaser. This tax is levied on the sale of goods, the provision of services and the importation of goods, by applying the tax rate to the price of such sales or services.

[344] However, VAT is not a cost for the purchaser since the VAT paid at the time the assets are purchased constitutes 'tax credit' and may be offset against the 'tax debit' derived from sales made or services rendered by the purchaser.

[345] The difference between the 'tax debit' and the 'tax credit', if it is positive, constitutes the amount to be paid to the tax authorities.

Turnover Tax

[346] Turnover tax is a local tax levied on the amount of gross income resulting from business activities carried out within the respective provincial jurisdictions. Normally, this tax is borne by the seller. Each of the provinces and the City of Buenos Aires applies different tax rates; however, most jurisdictions apply a 1% rate on agricultural, cattle breeding and mining activities, 1.5% on industrial activities, 3% on trade or services in general and 5.5% on financial activities.

Stamp Tax

[347] Stamp tax is a local tax levied on public or private instruments executed in Argentina or, if instruments are executed abroad, when such instruments are deemed to have effects in one or more relevant jurisdictions within Argentina. In general, this tax is calculated on the economic value of the agreement. Each jurisdiction applies different tax rates to different types of agreements, but the most common rate is 1%. Stamp tax is also applicable in the City of Buenos Aires.

[348] This tax is normally borne by both the buyer and the seller in equal amounts (50% each), but it is also a common business practice that the tax is borne by only one party (the buyer in most cases). In any case, the local tax authorities could claim the whole amount of the tax to either party because the law provides they are jointly liable.

Tax on Credits and Debits in Bank Accounts

[349] This tax is levied on debits and credits in bank accounts and on other transactions which, due to their special nature and characteristics, are similar to or could be used in substitution for a checking account, such as payments on behalf of or in the name of third parties, procedures for the collection of securities (*'valores'*) or documents, drafts and transfers of funds made by any means, when these transactions are performed by entities regulated by the Financial Entities Law No. 21,526.

[350] Transfers and deliveries of funds also fall within the scope of this tax, regardless of the person or entity that performs them, when those transactions are made through organized systems of payment in substitution for checking accounts.

[351] The general rate of the tax is 0.6%. An increased rate of 1.2% applies when there has been a substitution for the use of a checking account. And 33% of the tax paid by the owners of bank accounts may be used as payment on account of income tax. Also, 33% of the tax paid when there is a substitution of a bank account may be used as payment on account of income tax.

Tax-Free Reorganizations

[352] To encourage business reorganizations, the Income Tax Law provides that, in principle, corporate reorganizations shall not generate any tax liability, provided that specific conditions are satisfied.

Income Tax Law

[353] Income Tax Law establishes a tax-free reorganization regime according to which business reorganizations are not subject to income tax, and credits, tax losses and allowances may be transferred as a result of the transaction.

[354] For the purposes of Income Tax Law, a reorganization occurs when a merger, a division or spin-off, or a sale within the same economic group takes place. An economic group is deemed to exist if at least 80% of the capital of the transferee company belongs to the owners, partners or shareholders of the transferor company. In addition to these requirements, the owners, partners or shareholders of the transferor company must maintain in the transferee company at least 80% of the capital held by them at the time of the transfer.

[355] In order to qualify for the tax-free reorganization and to be able to transfer the tax status as a result of the transaction, the following requirements must be met:

(a) Continuance of activity: the companies must carry on the same or related activities as the previous companies for at least two years from the date of the reorganization. The date of the reorganization is understood as the date on which the continuing entity starts to carry on the same or related activities as those formerly carried on by the predecessor entities.
(b) Capital requirement: certain minimum percentages of capital maintenance in the new or absorbing company are required.

(c) Maintenance of capital: the amount of capital held in the new company on the date of the reorganization must be maintained for at least two years from that date. This requirement differs from the capital requirement in point (b) above, in that, in this case, the requirements refer to nominal amounts and not to a percentage participation in the capital of the new company.
(d) Activity: the companies must be active and pursuing their corporate objectives or purposes (not necessary in the case of sales within the same economic group).
(e) Same or related activities: the companies must have performed the same or related activities either during the twelve months preceding the date of the reorganization or the cessation of the activities, or during the months of the companies' existence if less than twelve months (not necessary in the case of sales within the same economic group).
(f) Report to the tax authorities: the reorganization must be reported to the federal tax authorities within 180 days from the reorganization date. The tax authorities' prior authorization is required when the reorganization does not involve a total transfer of assets, except for spin-offs.
(g) Capital requirement prior to the reorganization: in addition to the requirements mentioned above, there is a specific requirement for the transfer of losses and tax benefits arising from tax promotion regimes. The partners of the predecessor entities must have maintained, starting two years before the reorganization date or since the time of incorporation if such term is shorter, at least 80% of their participation in the capital of those entities. If this requirement is not met, the losses and some tax benefits are not transferred but the rest of the tax attributes are.

[356] If all the requirements mentioned above are met, the transaction qualifies as a tax-free reorganization. The main tax rights and allowances that are transferable to the new or absorbing company as a result of the merger are:

(a) Accumulated tax losses not barred by statute (i.e., whose deduction is specifically allowed).
(b) Balance of unamortized items for tax purposes.
(c) Balance of tax benefits and other special deductions and allowances not used by the previous company, and tax benefits granted under incentive legislation.
(d) Expenses deferred for tax purposes.
(e) Tax value of fixed assets, inventories and intangible assets, irrespective of the values assigned to them for the purpose of the transfer, and the basis for depreciation or amortization of fixed and intangible assets.
(f) Use of tax benefits received by the previous company as a result of sales, if tax rules provide for this.

Value Added Tax

[357] The VAT Law No. 23,349, as amended, provides that, for the purposes of this tax, transfers made as a result of a tax-free reorganization under the Income Tax Law are not considered sales. Therefore, reorganizations carried out according to the Income Tax Law are beyond the scope of VAT.

[358] The VAT Law also states that the tax balance of a company undergoing a reorganization may be transferred to the new or surviving companies. This means that the accumulated VAT credits that have not been offset up to the reorganization date may be transferred to the new or surviving company and offset against its accumulated VAT debits.

Turnover Tax

[359] Turnover tax is a local tax levied on gross income. Each of the provinces and the City of Buenos Aires apply different tax rates; however, most jurisdictions apply a 1% rate on agricultural, cattle breeding and mining activities, 1.5% on industrial activities, 3% on trade or services in general, and 5.5% on financial activities.

[360] As explained above, the tax is levied on the amount of gross income resulting from business activities carried out within the respective provincial jurisdictions. Some jurisdictions provide for tax exemption for corporate reorganizations that qualify as a tax-free reorganization under the Income Tax Law.

Stamp Tax

[361] Stamp tax is a local tax applicable on public or private instruments executed in Argentina or, if instruments are executed abroad, when such instruments are deemed to have effects in one or more relevant jurisdictions within Argentina. Stamp tax is also applicable in the City of Buenos Aires.

[362] Some jurisdictions provide for tax exemptions on reorganizations carried out pursuant to the tax-free company reorganization provisions of the Income Tax Law, provided certain requirements are met.

Transfer Pricing

[363] Local companies, trusts, permanent establishments and one-man companies are subject to transfer pricing regulations if they make business with related foreign individuals or entities or with entities situated in a low tax jurisdiction or a non-cooperative jurisdiction.

Non-cooperative jurisdictions are any jurisdiction or country that: (i) has not signed an information exchange agreement with Argentina; (ii) has not signed a convention to avoid double taxation with Argentina; or (iii) has signed either agreement or convention but does not comply with its obligation to share information with Argentina. The executive branch is responsible for issuing a list of non-cooperative jurisdictions.

Low tax jurisdiction includes any country, jurisdiction dominium, territory, associated state or special tax regime in which the maximum corporate income tax rate is lower than 60% of the income tax rate established in section 69 a) of the Income Tax Law. Therefore, to avoid being regarded as a low tax jurisdiction, the maximum corporate income tax rate of a given jurisdiction must be equal or higher than 18% during 2018 and 2019; and 15% starting on the year 2020. One of the main consequences of being regarded as a low tax jurisdiction is that funds transferred from such jurisdictions to an Argentine entity are considered untaxed income for the local entity, regardless of the nature of the funds, e.g. loan, capital contribution, etc.

[364] Article 15.1 of the Argentine Income Tax Law sets forth economic relationship as a parameter. Accordingly, two entities are related when they are controlled, directly or not, by the same legal entity, that can guide or define the activities of such entities, either by stock ownership, amount of credit due, influence or any other circumstances. The definition of the Argentine regulation is broader than the Organisation for Economic Co-operation and Development (OECD) guidelines.

EMPLOYMENT CONSIDERATIONS

Legislative Framework

[365] Most of the legal frameworks for labour contracts are provided by the Labour Contract Law (LCL). The main issues covered by the LCL include, but are not limited to: remuneration; annual vacations and special leaves of absence; holidays and non-working days; daily and weekly working and resting hours; special provisions for women and children; illness; and termination or transfer of a labour contract. These issues may not be modified by the parties if such amendments imply less favourable conditions to employees. In addition, each branch of industrial activity is governed as to wage scales and specific conditions by collective agreements negotiated between employers' associations and unions. There may also be special agreements executed between unions and specific companies.

[366] Furthermore, the parties may agree to specific individual conditions of employment by means of a written contract or a verbal agreement, provided they are more beneficial for the employees than the LCL or other applicable labour laws in general. Written contracts are frequent among key employees such as senior management, professionals and chief executive officers.

[367] Finally, it must be borne in mind that the customs and habits of a particular company may establish work practices which eventually become legally binding between the relevant parties and are thus a source of acquired rights.

Employment Protection

[368] The employer may terminate an employment relationship with or without cause. If the employer is ending the relationship without cause, the law provides that the employer must give appropriate prior notice of termination. If the relevant notice is not granted to the employee by the employer, the proportional amount of the employee's salary must be paid in lieu of such notice. The length of prior notice is dependent on the employee's tenure (one month's notice if the employee worked for the employer for less than five years and two months' notice if the employee worked for the employer for more than five years). Furthermore, the employer is obliged to pay to the employee any compensation to which he or she may be entitled, such as any outstanding wages, payment for vacation days, and the proportional entitlement to the '13th salary'. If prior notice is not given by the employer and the dismissal takes place on a day different from the last day of the month, the employee will collect, in addition to the prior notice, an amount equal to the salary corresponding to the remaining days of the month of dismissal.

[369] The employer is also required to pay compensation for seniority at the rate of one month's salary for each complete year of service performed, or period worked in excess of three months. The basis used for such severance calculation is the highest normal monthly salary earned during the previous year, or if the employee has worked less than a year, during his/her employment. If, however, the monthly salary (calculated as above) is higher than the ceiling figure provided by the relevant Collective Bargaining Agreement (CBA) applicable to the company at the time of the employee's dismissal, then this latter figure will be the one used for the calculation. However, the Argentine Supreme Court in re '*Vizzoti, Carlos v. AMSA S.A. on Dismissal*' declared the unconstitutionality of this cap when it resulted in a reduction of the monthly salary calculation bases of more than 33% and thus stated that the calculation basis could not be lower than 67% of the best remuneration of the dismissed employee. However, in no case can the severance payment be less than one full monthly salary.

[370] According to the full bench decision '*Tulosai, Alberto Pascual v. Central Bank of the Republic of Argentina on Law 25 561*', thirteenth salary and non-monthly performance bonuses shall not be included in the calculation basis for compensation for seniority unless, in the case of performance bonuses, fraud was proved to exist, in which case voluntary bonuses might, subject to case-by-case analysis, impact the severance calculation.

[371] Special severance packages exist for certain situations, such as a dismissal on account of pregnancy, marriage or on account of the employee's race, colour, religion, sex, national origin or handicap, or if the employee is a union representative or is in a public office.

[372] The severance amounts must be paid to the employee in a lump sum payment within four working days of dismissal. However, the parties may agree otherwise in writing through the execution of a settlement agreement before the Labour Secretary. In Argentina it is advisable to enter into settlement and release agreements that, once approved by the Labour Secretary, have res judicata effects and minimize the risk of future claims. If the employer is terminating the relationship with just cause, no severance or prior notice need to be granted to the dismissed employee. However, the employer must take extreme care in advance to verify the seriousness of the infringement by the employee, especially considering the highly employee-protective tendencies of Argentine labour courts. Dismissals for cause may trigger severance, fines and damages, and are subject to a very high and strict test of acceptance and validity.

[373] The LCL establishes that the employer may dismiss an employee for force majeure and economic reasons, in which cases the employer may pay employees an amount equal to 50% of regular severance. An employer may also dismiss employees if work cannot be carried out for reasons outside the control of the employer which could not be avoided with reasonable care (even if not technically force majeure). The employer must prove that it has not been responsible for the job loss and must be able to reasonably justify its actions. The employer must be able to show that the event will have a lasting effect and that it inevitably led to the dismissals. Dismissals must take place in the order ascending tenure and, regarding employees with similar hire dates, in consideration of dependent relatives. The employer must act with extreme caution when deciding to apply this reduced severance alternative, as judges are reluctant to validate it and, if unsuccessful, severance differences, fines and damages may be triggered.

[374] Under Argentine law, whenever the employer is in the need to dismiss or suspend employees as a result of force majeure, or economic or technological reasons and such dismissals or suspensions affect a certain percentage of employees, a special procedure called the Crisis Prevention Procedure ('CPP') must be followed before the Labour Secretary. Under the CPP, the parties must try to negotiate solutions to the conflict and try to avoid terminations or suspensions. Our interpretation is that the CPP should only apply when terminations are structured in the reduced severance scenario mentioned above. However, a broad interpretation by local authorities considers that the CPP might be considered applicable if a significant number of employees are dismissed, even where full severance is paid.

[375] Amounts received pursuant to severance packages are considered taxable according to the Income Tax Law, except compensation paid for seniority. However, the Supreme Court of Justice had declared that the compensation derived from the termination of the employment relationship is not under the scope of tax as it is considered as an income that it is not likely to have periodicity nor is its source permanent, which are conditions for the application of the tax. The 'Negri' ruling takes the reasoning upheld in the 'De Lorenzo' case further recalled in the 'Cuevas' case.

[376] In all these cases the Supreme Court established the non-taxability of the concepts received by the employee on the termination of the employment relationship for lack of regularity and permanence of source. This line of reasoning has the approval of the Argentine Attorney General's Office, who originally initiated this reasoning. Case law mentioned hereinabove was finally observed by the Federal Tax Authority (FTA) since such organism enacted internal dispositions in this respect.

[377] On a recent development, a tax reform introduced in December 2017 through Law No. 27,430, which was then regulated by Decree No 976/2018, partially affected and modified the tax treatment for terminations with regards to senior executives. According to Law No. 27,430, any amount paid on top of statutory severance to employees in director and executive positions, as such positions were subsequently defined and regulated, would now be subject to income tax.

[378] Decree No. 976/2018 provided the required regulation and, without full clarity and subject to several interpretations, provided two elements to define the universe of employees whose amounts paid on top of statutory severance would be taxable, as follows: (i) the employee's monthly salary must exceed fifteen times the General Minimum Statutory Salary; and (ii) the employee must have been in board of directors or in other boards or similar committees that implement shareholders or other policies, at least within the last twelve months of employment, continuously or not. These parameters will be narrowed and more accurately defined in the coming years, if and when presented to the FTA or competent courts for analysis. This special situation presents the dual risk that the approach taken by employers may expose them to claims by the FTA (if no withholding is made) or by the dismissed employee in a labour court (if taxes are actually withheld).

Change of Employment Conditions

[379] Any change of employment conditions which adversely affects employees will, in principle, entitle the employees to either: (i) consider themselves constructively dismissed and claim severance payment; or (ii) to initiate legal actions seeking the court to restore former labour conditions.

Joint Labour Responsibility During Acquisition Procedures

[380] As we mentioned above in 'Labour and Social Security Aspects', on the obligations arising from the labour relationship, the law imposes a joint and several liability on the seller and the buyer. Case law has, in certain cases, even extended the buyer's liability to the labour and social security obligations of employees whose labour relationships with the former employer were terminated prior to the transfer.

[381] In view of the joint and several liabilities that arise as a result of a transfer, it is common for the seller and buyer to make special provisions between them as to who should bear these liabilities. These agreements are, however, only valid as agreements between the parties, and do not have any effect in respect of either the employees concerned or the social security authorities.

Working Day Law

[382] The workday not only includes the time effectively worked but also the time the worker is at the employer's disposal.

The Working Day Law No. 11,544 ('WDL') sets forth that:

> The duration of the work shall not exceed 8 daily hours or 48 weekly hours for any person hired in private or public entities, *regardless if such entities are non profit organizations. The limitation set forth by this law is the maximum and it does not prevent such entities from setting a lower duration than 8 daily hours or 48 weekly hours.*

[383] A workday may be established in any of the following ways: limiting the work day so that it does not exceed eight hours per day or forty-eight hours a week, as long as work duties on Saturdays end at 1 p.m.; or uneven distribution of the forty-eight hours among the working days of the week, when work days of one or more days last less than eight hours. The extra time of the other days may not exceed an hour a day and activity on Saturdays must still end at 1 p.m. Night shifts, which are defined as those worked between 9 p.m. and 6 a.m., may not exceed seven hours and employees who work shorter night shifts must collect the same salary as employees who work the longer day shifts.

[384] With regards to the hours worked in excess of the legal working day, the LCL sets forth that:

> The employer shall pay to the employee who renders services during overtime a fifty percent (50%) surcharge calculated on the regular salary, if such time involves week days, and of one hundred percent (100%) if such time involves Saturdays after 1:00 p.m., Sundays and legal holidays.

[385] The provisions of WDL concerning limit of hours worked, and thus eligibility to overtime payments, are not applicable to 'directors' and 'managers'. Similar to our discussion above regarding income tax executive positions, it is not clear whether the scope of the term applies to 'directors' and 'managers', although it is generally accepted to refer to top executives within the structure of a company. In any event, even if no hour limits apply, there must be at least a twelve-hour break between one work day and the following, as with any other employee.

Pensions

[386] The age of retirement for employees is 65 for men and 60 for women. The employer may demand employees to file for retirement but, regardless of the statutory retirement age, the employer's demand may only be issued when the employee is 70 years old, assuming the worker also meets the number of service years required by law (i.e. thirty, except for special situations). After lawfully sending this demand for retirement, the employer is under an obligation to maintain the labour relationship until either the employee begins to receive pension benefits from his or her pension fund or after one year has passed, whichever occurs earlier.

Retention of Key Management and Employees

[387] With a labour market that allows employees to move from job to job more easily, retention bonuses have provided a great way for companies to keep valuable employees. Retention bonuses are payments or rewards that are different from the employee's regular salary that is offered as an incentive to keep a key employee on the job during a particularly crucial business cycle, like a merger or acquisition, or during a crucial production period. In recent years, retention bonuses have become increasingly popular and have proven to be a very good tool in persuading employees to stay.

Non-compete Agreements and Confidentiality

Non-compete

[388] An employee has a duty of loyalty to the employer and is barred from engaging in competitive activities during the period of his/her employment. Furthermore, key employees are normally required by their contracts to work exclusively and upon a full-time basis for their employers.

[389] The above obligations, however, expire once the labour relationship has terminated. Contractual stipulations providing that the employee will not compete after the termination of the labour contract are of doubtful validity under Argentine law since they are considered to conflict with the provision in the Constitution which provides that all persons have an unfettered right to work. For such reason, case law has considered that a reasonable time limitation should exist, which has been considered of up to two years. However, it has also been considered by case law that for this non-compete clause to be enforceable certain compensation should be paid to the former employee to cover his or her inability to obtain another job in the industry where he or she worked for his or her former employer.

Confidentiality

[390] The employee's duty to keep company secrets continues during the period of employment and extends indefinitely beyond the end of that period. The employee will therefore always be under an obligation not to reveal confidential information or company secrets.

Non-solicitation

[391] Similar to a non-compete, a non-solicitation agreement is a form of restrictive covenant, which constitutes a clause in an employment contract or post-employment agreement restricting the employee, directly or indirectly, individually or through any person, from hiring any employee or consultant from the company that they have worked for. This commitment may also be extensible to the request of customers or other business opportunities, making this obligation even more restrictive under risk of affecting the worker's right and freedom to work.

[392] As well as non-compete covenants, non-solicitation covenants are being used by companies in order to prevent those former key employees from affecting their competitive activities. For this reason, the non-solicitation clauses may need to be clearly and carefully drafted to become enforceable as well as limited in time.

[393] Given the lack of any legal provisions, the obligations under non-solicitation clauses are of doubtful enforceability but subject to the guidelines for enforceability applicable to non-compete agreements.

Treatment of Foreign Employees

[394] The Argentine Constitution grants all residents of Argentina, regardless of their nationality, the right to work; that is why Argentine entities are fully authorized to receive and hire expatriate or otherwise foreign employees at their discretion and with no limitation in number. Nevertheless, foreigners who wish to work in Argentina must first obtain a transitory or temporary residency permit, depending upon the amount of time they plan to spend in the country and on their nationality.

[395] In an ordinary process, the request for any form of residence permit must be preceded by the issue of an entrance permit (*Permiso de Ingreso*) by the Immigration Department (*Dirección Nacional de Migraciones*), which is requested by the to-be employer. However, the request for a residence may also be filed with the Immigration Department directly by the foreigner.

[396] *Transitory Residency Visa*: A residence permit is required for a person who wishes to stay for a period of time of fewer than three months and may classify for such visa.

[397] *Temporary Residency Visa*: This type of residence permit is valid for a year and can be renewed upon three occasions to take its duration up to three years.

[398] *Business Visas:* They are issued for specific short term assignments, with a maximum of ninety days and may be extended for additional ninety days. Business visas may be applied for at the Argentine consulate with jurisdiction over the applicant's home country. The process may have to be initiated in Argentina if there is an Argentine inviting company.

[399] *Temporary Residency for Mercosur Natives (Patria Grande)*: The Immigration Department stated a special programme for foreign residents who are natives of the states of Mercosur and its associated states (Uruguay, Paraguay, Brazil, Colombia, Bolivia, Chile, Peru, Ecuador and Venezuela). This programme simplified the proceedings to obtain a temporary residence; it can be requested in the Republic of Argentina and its validity is for two years.

[400] It is very important to carefully and thoroughly review the compensation package, benefits and work tools of an expatriate to assess the registration obligations, remuneration treatment and associated formalities and risks.

FUTURE DEVELOPMENTS

[401] In October 2019 new presidential elections will take place in the country. President Macri will seek re-election to a second term, in which his administration will try to maintain the direction led during the last three years; that is to say, revitalizing Argentina's economy with free-market reforms and improving international relations.

[402] As explained above, the Macri administration has put the emphasis on market-oriented reforms, liberalizing trade and lifting several foreign exchange controls imposed by the former administration. In this new context, we expect that M&A related work will be very active in the coming years.

[illegible]

[illegible]

FUTURE DEVELOPMENTS

[illegible]

[illegible]

Made in the USA
Monee, IL
13 September 2026

62974275R00046